THE WITHDRAWAL OF HUMAN PROJECTION

*A Study of Culture and
Internalized Objects*

THE WITHDRAWAL OF HUMAN PROJECTION

A Study of Culture and Internalized Objects

M.D. Faber

The Library of Art and Social Science
New York

LCN: 89-80571
ISBN: 0-915042-21-5

Manufactured in the United States of America

Designed and Computer Typeset by
Dorothy Wasserman Associates, Inc.
New York City

Table Of Contents

Forward and Acknowledgements

Part One: The Transitional Nature of Ordinary Consciousness
1. The Process of Mind-Body Conversion   1
2. From the Cradle   3
3. The Internalization of the World   4
4. The Mirror   6
5. The Dark Side of the Mirror:Splitting   8
6. The Agony of Differentiation   11
7. The Sands of Time and the Container of Space   13
8. The Stimulus Itself   15
9. The Word   16
10. The Tie to the Culture   18
11. The Oedipus, and After   22
Notes and References Part One   25

Part Two: The Cultural Sphere
1. Some Background   29
2. The Religio-Economic Realm   38
3. Money and Magna Mater   41
4. The Sacrificial Way to the Object   44
5. Sacred Lucre   47
6. Psychodynamic Extrapolations   49
7. The Metaphors of Marx   52
8. The Interest in Interest   57
9. The Vicious Circle and the Bad Parent   59
10. More Opiates, More Anxieties   62
11. Lurking Ambivalence   66
12. Goods and More Goods   69
Notes and References Part Two

Part Three: Disrupting the Tie to the Inner World
1. A Glance Backward, A Glance Forward   79
2. The Meaning of Non-Ordinary Moments   81
3. The Emergence of the Non-Ordinary World   84
4. Solidifying One's Change   89
5. Transforming the Past at the Mind-Body Level   91
Notes and References Part Three   98

Forward and Acknowledgements

What follows is an attempt to present in relatively brief compass a psychoanalytic theory of individual and group behavior. Worked out over the years in a variety of articles and books, the theory strives to illustrate the manner in which the psychosomatically experienced internal objects of infancy and childhood get transformed into cultural ideas. The theory is perceptual as well as psychological, and I frequently employ the word "perception" to indicate this; yet I am not unaware of the difficulties and imperfections of such an employment. The object of the early period enters the perceptual apparatus at a deep psychological level that cannot be understood in isolation from the physiological realities of the organism. At the same time, I do not wish to suggest that physiological factors rigidly determine the nature of psychological motivation and response. To delete the physiological dimension feels wrong. To include it feels provisional in that science has not yet made clear exactly where the physiological and psychological meet, let alone how they meet, and what it all means with regard to the possibilities for individual and social change. I would like to think my analyses contribute something to the dialogue.

On many occasions I put words and phrases between inverted commas to indicate a double meaning, a rich metaphoric and psychoanalytic significance that underlies the basic denotation. My purpose is simply to get more from these materials and from the passages and analyses that surround them than I would otherwise get. For example, the word "structural" suggests both the individual's place in a corporate structure of the economy and the way this may reflect specific structural issues of life's first years, or the structure of the psyche. Similarly, the word "part" can indicate both segment and part object; the word "position" can indicate both the reality of an occupation and the position of the child in the family; the word "incorporate" can indicate both the economic procedure and the psychological tendency to merge, or cross ego boundaries. Needless to say, I want this tactic to be stimulating and pleasurable rather than annoying.

I want also to stress that my final section does not offer relaxation techniques, and in particular meditative concentration, as an ameliorative procedure that stands apart from strong and persistent psychoanalytic understanding. Reason and insight are as important to my method of change as are quieting the body and emptying the mind.

i

Moments of relaxation will be informed at a deep, silent level of awareness by knowledge of the psychological sources of one's stress. The rational, analytic grasp of one's stress will be supplemented and enhanced by a bodily practice of detachment that offers a new perceptual outlook on creation. In short, the aim is to grasp discursively what cuts us off from the world and stifles our healing interaction with others, and to prepare our tense, miserable bodies, our dulled and damaged organs of perception, for a fresh and healthful participation in the environment. Moreover, I am not suggesting in my final section that what I call our transitional mode of awareness will suddenly cease through employment of this two-sided program. My method is, ultimately, *an example of a method* that strives to diminish the perceptual tie to the object, and I offer it in that spirit. I am not absolutely certain how one goes about diminishing the influence of internalized objects on perception. I am certain only that such influence must be diminished, and I grope in a way that will hopefully be useful to others. My cherished wish is that people begin to think about this in earnest.

I would like to express my indebtedness to Dr. Richard A. Koenigsberg of the Library of Social Science, New York. Not only did Dr. Koenigsberg's assistance make this work possible, but his insights and suggestions along the way greatly enriched my understanding. Finally, I wish to acknowledge the outstanding secretarial help that I received from Ms. Colleen Donnelly of the English Department, University of Victoria.

Part One

The Transitional Nature
of Ordinary Consciousness

1. The Process of Mind-Body Conversion

My thesis is radical, perhaps startling, and certainly basic to psychological growth and change: our ordinary consciousness, our ordinary, everyday awareness of ourselves and of the world around us, is a major source of our alienation and stress. Moreover, what we take for granted as our normal mentation and perception is a major source of global suffering and upheaval in the form of injustice, exploitation, cruelty, and war. It is enormously difficult for us to see this because our ordinary consciousness is designed to serve a defensive purpose. I mean, it is designed in significant measure to shield us from deep, genuine realization of our insecurity. It has been built up over the years to protect us from specific emotional experiences that are rooted in life's early, formative stages and that are kept alive at the mind-body level by our persistent unconscious anxiety.

While it may be true to say that the defensive function of ordinary consciousness works, or works for the vast majority of "adjusted" human beings, it is also true to say that it works at a tremendous price: it prevents us from developing our full potential as sentient, relational beings; it makes us creatures of mental habit, inflexible creatures whose existence oscillates between an adaptive familiarity and sameness of perception on the one hand, and an anxious sense of alteration and danger on the other; and most of all, it predisposes us to indulge our capacity for projective identification, for attributing to the external world, including of course the other people therein, our own deeply buried inclinations and fears and then interacting with the world on that basis.[1] What is particularly nefarious about projective identification is that it prompts the recipient of the projection to react in a manner that confirms the projecter's delusional thinking; in this way, it expands the sphere of mutually destructive relations and deepens the irrationality of the environment in which we exist.

The upshot? What we take to be, and accept as, "reality" is not given, inherited, somehow presented to us by the universe. It is *made*. It is made from the very inception of our lives by our active, projecting minds. Indeed, our "reality" is commensurate with our past experience,

1

with the manner in which we responded to the events that comprised our emotional and perceptual lives. Thus our egos, our perceptual apparatuses, are not neutral. On the contrary, they are *loaded*, and the beginning of genuine psychological growth is to *see* this. What is closest to us, what we take for granted, what is ostensibly transparent, normal, given, namely our very mode of perception (and, as we shall see, the cultural configurations that result from it) is what is most elusive, difficult, opaque, and even sinister precisely because it has been unconsciously designed *not to be revealed in its defensive capacity.* It "works" because it is not analyzed; it "works" because we do not turn toward it but away from it as we employ it unthinkingly in the so-called real world. It keeps us from those things we imagine to be terrible (they are not in actual fact so terrible) and we persist in the arrangement for infantile reasons. We choose not to face again the anxiety of the early years, and yet we remain in an ordinary consciousness that has precisely the anxious tension of those years embedded inextricably within it.

I want to drive toward the essence of the matter by declaring that what we consider to be our normal, ordinary awareness is in fact a *conversion symptom.* The term "conversion" was introduced into developmental psychology by Freud and his followers toward the turn of the century. It denotes the capacity of the human being to convert traumatic ideas or thoughts into bodily forms of expression which are unconsciously and pathologically designed to render the thoughts and ideas harmless. For example, one of Freud's first patients, a woman he called Anna O, underwent a paralysis of the arm whenever her buried feelings toward her father were aroused. The paralysis desisted as unconscious materials were brought to light. The "conversion," Freud maintained, might be partial or total, and although it allowed the individual "to resolve the incompatability within himself" it also burdened him with a kind of "memory-symbol," or "parasite," in the form of a bodily innervation.[2]

Freud's interests eventually led him away from study of the body's recording of emotional disorders. A number of his followers, however, pursued the matter vigorously. What they concluded has been generally accepted by the psychological community and may be summarized as follows: There are no purely somatic processes in human life, even from the beginning. At every stage of his development the human creature is a psycho-physical entity in which bodily and emotional processes are fused.[3] To speak of the mind apart from the body is as incorrect as to speak of the body apart from the mind. This means that psychic stress, whatever its origin, will leave its mark upon the body, will be registered there. Freud's "conversion process" is a universal aspect of human development because human development always involves emotional stress and because emotional stress always begets physiological expression. It is not only the neurotic symptom of the disturbed individual (compulsively washing one's hands, for example) that we must regard as a "compromise formation,"[4] as a method of fending off anxiety, of coping with psychological tension. The behavior of each and every person reveals compromise formations and attests to his having answered the anxieties and tensions of his life through the conversion process. Neurosis is simply an exaggerated version of what we take to be normal conduct. Now, when one considers that perception is as much a behavior as maintaining a certain posture, or eating, or making love, when one returns, in short, to the basic premise that the human creature is a psycho-physical entity, one confronts the radical and startling contention with which I opened this section and which I mean to illustrate henceforward: our ordinary consciousness, our ordinary way of perceiving and being-in the world, is itself a conversion symptom, a witness to the strains and imperfections of our past and present life.

2. From the Cradle

Until recently, babies were routinely operated upon without anesthetics because the doctors believed the babies did not feel pain. Astounding as that may seem it is not untypical of the ignorance and insensitivity that westerners have displayed toward infants over the centuries. If the reader has an appetite for this horror story, I refer him to the work of those psycho-historians who have been devoting themselves to the subject for about thirty years.[5] Although the mistreatment of babies is still a common occurrence, and may always be common given the tendency of human beings to transfer their own frustrations and discontentments to their offspring, we are at last beginning to grasp in some depth what might be called the nature of the infant's special world.

This is, of course, a huge subject. But what is crucial to bear in mind here is that 1) by two weeks babies can look, listen, and even imitate the facial gestures of their parents;[6] 2) by ten weeks infant memory is robust, and it steadily improves during the next few months. The young infant, writes Kail, "is an unexpectedly capable memorizer;"[7] 3) by eighteen months infants begin to mnemically economize--that is, they begin to construct "general representations of experience that integrate the important features of individual experiences;"[8] 4) the associations and dreams of people undergoing deep psychotherapy are often filled with materials from the first months and years of life;[9] and finally, 5) specialists in the development of the human mind-brain agree that the mind as we know it is born in and through the baby's initial interactions with the environment and in particular with the caretaker(s). The basis of mind is cultural, not individual. Mind is born early in life "as an infant is attracted to sources of comfort and repelled by sources of distress."[10]

One of the most remarkable facts brought to light by the developmental psychology of our era is the extent to which our intellectual and emotional lives are determined by what happens to us during our first five or six years. Our early interrelational experience becomes the scaffolding on which our subsequent characters are built. The whole perceiving organism, the very essence of the emerging mind-body, is the product of its first interactions with the world. While we must not "adultomorphize" the baby, while we must not "read into" its existence adult recognitions and responses, we must also not fail to discern the perdurable significance of the early period, for in grasping that, in seeing that, and in connecting it to our present attitudes and tendencies, we provide ourselves with a huge, potential source of liberation.

3.   The Internalization of the World

It boils down to this: from the very beginning of our existence we *internalize* the world; we take experiential events into our emerging mind-body, and we do this fully, deeply, and finally at the level of ganglionic-snyaptic development itself. If the reader is wondering why the early period is so crucial, so all-determining for our later lives, this is where the answer begins to emerge, in the psychodynamics of human internalization. Even when we are thinking logically as adults, even when we are indulging in the"pure reason" that we associate with philosophers such as Descartes and Kant, the legacy of our early years is there, humming beneath the surface, as it were. If one can think of the multi-faceted human ego as a group of actors standing upon a stage, one will understand "pure reason" as a mental request that everyone move out of the way so that "reason" may preside at the center. The cooperative members of the cast may do this, *but they do not leave the stage*, and they *influence* "reason" by their continual presence there. The living organism, in other words, always *perceives* the world with the whole mind, as opposed to thinking about it with only a part of the mind. Perception, not thinking, is primary. To choose still another metaphor, our peripheral emotional vision is never absent. That is why we can reason coldly and behave quite passionately all in the same *perceptual* moment. We are the animal that thinks while it shoots, or drops bombs. We are the animal that is characterized by "splitting," by the radical compartmentalizing of whole sides of our personalities and the "acting-out" that accompanies such a self-alienating procedure. Of the powerful internalizing that we do toward the inception of our lives, that which involves the caretaker (usually the mother) is of enormous significance. As developmental psychologists express it, the *object* (this term is used because the caretaker is not yet perceived by the baby as a person) enters the infant's dawning psyche as the deep internalization of life's earliest phase, and she persists there as a presence, later to become an image during the period in which verbalization begins.[11] This interplay between mother and infant is directly involved in the shaping of the infant's personality. Intuitive or feeling perception begins with maximal intensity at birth as the baby becomes subject in a structuring way to the maternal attitude. During life's first weeks and months the infant and its caregiver are locked in a symbiotic relationship the intensity of which can hardly be overstated. True, we come naked into this world, and we come separate into it, unattached to others of our kind except in the very rare instance of Siamese twins. But this, our primal condition, is belied by the relational field, the field of the *object*, in which we discover ourselves from the moment of our birth. We leave the total maternal symbiosis of the womb to enter the almost total symbiosis of the first relationship. In contrast to the African wildebeest which is on its feet and perhaps running for its life only hours after emerging from its mother, the human infant enters the scene in a totally helpless, dependent condition, and he remains in that condition for a considerable period. In a very real way, he is nurtured into existence as a person through his intensive symbiotic contact with his parent.[12] Thus our separateness, our sense of ourselves as individuals, is something that we gradually achieve over a relatively long period of five or six years. So intense, so pervasive, and so basic is this interaction between mother and child that we would do well to regard the mother herself not as a distinct entity but as a kind of organ of the baby. It is in the growth of this unique union that we find the nucleus of human identity.

4. The Mirror

The genesis and the formation of the self derive from the baby's initial mirroring experience with the mother.[13] For the past few decades this remarkable aspect of our origins has been studied intensively and has come to be regarded as a central feature of our development.[14] The investigations of Rene Spitz and his associates during the 1950's and 1960's established at the clinical level the baby's inclination to concentrate on the mother's face--and in particular on her eyes--during periods of feeding. For three, or perhaps four months the nursing infant does not look at the mother's breast (or at the bottle held close to her breast) but at her face. "From the moment the mother comes into the room to the end of nursing he stares at her face."[15] What is especially interesting in this regard is the connection between such primal gazing and the mouth, or "oral cavity."

While the child takes into his mouth and body his physical nourishment, he takes into his dawning awareness or his "visceral brain" the emotional, psychological materials that he discovers in the face, eyes, and bodily attitude of the mother. It is often remarked that the first ego is a "body ego" and that our later life is influenced at the perceptual level by the foundational experiences our bodies undergo as consciousness awakens.[16] We have here a compelling instance of how this works. When Spitz calls the "oral cavity" in its conjunction with the mother's body "the cradle of human perception," he reminds us that sucking in and spitting out are the first, the most basic, and the most persistent perceptual behaviors among humans.They underlie at the bodily level our subsequent rejections and acceptances, our subsequent negations and celebrations, of experience.

Although Spitz established the baby's inclination to stare at the mother's face, he did not state that mother and infant spend considerable time looking at each other, nor did he contend that such looking, along with the mother imitating the infant's facial expressions and sounds, provided the means for the baby to regard the mother's face and sounds as his own.[17] An inborn tendency on the part of the infant prompts him to seek out his mother's gaze and to do so regularly and for extended periods. The mother, because of tendencies developed during the course of her relationship with her own mother, sets about exploiting this mutual face-gazing activity. As the eye to eye contact becomes frequent, and easily observed by the investigator, the mother's inclination to continually change her facial expression, as well as the quality of her vocalizing, emerges with striking clarity. Usually she smiles and nods and coos; sometimes in response to an infant frown she frowns. In virtually every instance the mother's facial and vocal behavior comprises an imitation of the baby's. Thus, as the mother descends to the infant's level she provides him with a particular kind of human reflection. She does not simply give the baby back his own self; she reinforces a portion of the baby's behavior in comparison with another portion. She gives the baby back not merely a part of what he is doing but in addition something of her own. In individual development, "the precursor of the mirror is the mother's face."[18] The upshot may be stated as follows: the kind of behavior we connect with the ego or the perceptual apparatus derives in large measure from the behavior of the mother. Not only does she trigger the ego's formation, she determines the kind of stimuli to which the child will attend, including the stimuli that will eventually come through language.

The entire developmental sequence has been captured in detail by Daniel Stern.[19] For the infant, hundreds of "experiential units" are strung together and occur over and over again during each interaction, every day. The infant has the opportunity to internalize each "unit" as a separate representation. At the level of neuronic processes, of course, these internalizations become an integral part of the human mind-brain. In other words, they trigger memory traces and get stored. For a "unit" to become internalized there must be a physical, a cognitive, and an emotional aspect to the experience. When these are in place assimilation occurs. At the foundational level of our perceptual nature, cognition and emotion cannot be treated separately, compartmentalized. We begin and we continue as human beings to "see the world feelingly," as Gloucester puts it in *King Lear*. Although such feeling may be scarcely discernable, or even totally concealed by one's attitude toward the world, it is there.

Our mental makeup, then, is shaped by those with whom we entered into "object relations" during the early phases of our development. Our earliest "objects" become dynamic parts of our personality structure and continue to influence us in all that we do long after the specific persons who were the aim of our internalizing tendency have ceased to be. By the time we have reached adulthood there exists within us an inner world, a kind of psychic universe which is inhabited by the "objects" that have entered us, or more properly, that we have taken into ourselves along our maturational way. We live in two worlds, from the beginning, and our perceptual life must be regarded as a function of the interaction of these worlds which continually impinge upon one another.

5.   The Dark Side of the Mirror: Splitting

We are beginning to understand the psychological direction from which ordinary awareness arises. To do this more fully, however, we must grasp the two-sided, or "split" nature of our early, foundational experience. On the one hand, many of the "representational units" which the baby takes in contribute to his contentment. The mother gives him a positive, nurturing introduction to existence. She soothes him, reassures him, delights him; she develops his confidence, his enthusiasm, his "joy in life." In a word, she triggers his participation in "good" materials.

On the other hand, many of the "units" that are assimilated by the growing child are disruptive, or, in a very special sense, *negative* in quality. This becomes particularly true as the mirror phase blends into the phase in which the child is able to recognize himself as a separate creature, separate that is from the caretaking parent upon whom his existence depends. Needless to say, this phase is essential to our actualization as higher organisms, for it is only with the development of the capacity to create a mental representation of the absent object that the child progresses from the immediate, sensory response to the delayed, conceptual response that is characteristically human.[20] Just as the occurrence of birth involves trauma, trauma that some believe permanently marks the organism,[21] so does the early relationship with the mother. Even the most normally endowed child, with the most optimally available mother, is unable to weather the separation process without crisis, or to emerge into the next phase of development unscathed.[22] As Michael Eigen expresses it, "fragmentation and division are as much a part of our starting point as union and continuity."[23] I will concentrate in what follows on the way in which the "anxiety units" of the early time find their way to the ground of our perception and thus trigger the conversion process described toward the beginning of the discussion.

As the child goes about building up his good maternal representation, as he gradually enlarges those aspects of the caretaker that will serve as the perceptual basis for his positive participation in the world, he confronts of necessity the imperfections of the symbiotic relationship in which he is involved. No matter how solicitous the mother is, the infant is fated to undergo tension, frustration, discomfort, and even a certain amount of pain. Such experiences mobilize anxiety. Indeed, very young infants display identical patterns of anxious behavior when they discover themselves in frightening situations, and when they are in contact with the caretaker during a period in which she is tense, angry, disquieted, or anxious herself.[24] Repeated, inescapable exposure to inconsistent conduct prompts the developing baby to *split* the caretaker into what are customarily called in psychological circles a "good" and a "bad object" and to *internalize* these objects into a part or aspect of his perceiving self. The collection of people which each of us harbors within, carries about, and projects into our reality, reaches back in every instance to the first pair of our personifications: the good mother and the bad or evil mother. With the passage of time these early, primitive personifications get transmuted into the good me, the bad me, and the ambiguous, dreadful not me.

We must remember here that the mother's inconsistency is a grave, disruptive event for the child, that it corresponds to his worst imaginings and fears. The postponement of gratification from its mother's supplies constitutes for the infant a trauma, and residues of the infant's reaction to this trauma can be found in the psychology of later years.[25] Because he is simply not able to *integrate* the mother's two sides, her "bad" and "good" aspects, the infant attempts to *coordinate* them by splitting and then dealing with the splits. He declares, in effect, "*mother* is not bad. There just happens to be this bad mother who appears once in a while. She and mother are not really the same person, for *mother* is always good and will never hurt and disappoint. I am obliged to interact with both *mother* and the other one" (author's quotation). Only later, when the child matures, will he be able to accept "goodness and badness" in the *same* person.[26]

Thus threats to the narcissistic integrity of the self, or to our primitive emotional and bodily self-esteem, exist from the moment of birth and stem from the interaction of the child's wishes and needs with the demands and frustrations of the external world. Such narcissistic wounds may evoke feelings of depression and a growing sense of perplexity that is frequently answered with aggressive behavior.[27] The infant's mere inability to influence, predict, or comprehend an event which he expected on the basis of his previous experience to be able to control or understand is registered as trauma.[28] Because the infant's thought, the whole of his primitive mentation, is tied inextricably to the mother, her mere absence through temporary departure can leave the infant with the terrible feeling that he is *empty*, empty in his mind and emotions.[29] We may have here the deep origin and most basic, enduring expression of the feeling that one is "losing one's mind." We also now realize that the parents' very power over the life and death of the child is perceived as threatening, and internalized to become part of everyone's susceptibility to nightmare, everyone's residual paranoia.[30] Odd as it may sound to express it this way, merely being born human is a major source of stress.

The Jungian researches of Erich Neumann are helpful on this score. The symbolism of the "Terrible Mother," he writes, draws its images from the inside. That is, the "bad object" appears in fantastic, ghastly forms that do not originate in the environment. Whether we are in "Egypt or India, Mexico or Etruria, Bali or Rome," we confront the archetypal expression of these intra-psychic "monsters." In the tales and myths of "all peoples, ages, and countries," as well as in our own nightmares, "witches, vampires, ghouls and spectres assail us, all terrifyingly alike."[31] It is the internalizing of this bad object that explains our emotional fear of death. At issue here is not death as the adult conceives it, but a threat of a quality and magnitude beyond the adult's imagination. We get a glimpse of it in states of panic and in the momentary probe into infancy that some individuals experience during the course of psychotherapy. Thus the struggle between the forces of life and death which is inherent in the biologically precarious infantile condition becomes involved in the infant's response to the mother that protects and satisfies and to the mother that frustrates and deprives.[32] Where the fear of death is concerned, it is the uncertain ties to the living world at all ages that shake us more than the awareness of biological cessation.[33]

What I am maintaining is that we cannot understand the complex symbol that death comprises for the human creature if we exclude from the discussion the primal anxiety of the early period. Because the mother's impact on the child is pre-verbal, because her presence is internalized before higher conceptualization begins, it is very, very difficult to subject our split foundations to reason. Our anxious obsession with death, as well as our dangerous indulgence in rigid, dichotomous views of the world, with the "good guys" over here and the "bad guys" over there,[34] is rooted largely in a primitive, defensive splitting that leaves perdurable traces on our "normal" perception.

6. The Agony of Differentiation

As the child begins to separate from the parent in earnest, further splitting, further enhancement of the bad object occurs. The symbiosis of the very early period may have been imperfect, but it was there, and it reassured the baby in his precarious infantile condition. Now that is taken away. In grasping the effect of this, we must bear in mind that for the infant the repeated association of the perception of the mother and the relief of tension creates in itself an emotional investment in the mother. Separation involves trauma because the maternal figure is recognized as separate *only* as the infant experiences frustration and need. In this way, separation comes to mean disappointment.[35]

To express the matter from another angle, because the infant's attachment is there before the other is experienced as other, the growing awareness of the caretaker as a differentiated being is itself experienced as a loss. True, there is a gain in cognitive comprehension as this proceeds. At the same time, however, there is the awareness that certain treasured sensations are not part of the self but can come and go.[36] Thus the presence of the early, powerful attachment both facilitates and complicates our movement away from the mother, our growth as separate, differentiated creatures. It facilitates by providing us with a stable, loving internalization that endures and that leads us toward positive attachment to other people. It complicates because the experience of loss permanently endows the relationship to the mother with painful undercurrents and sets up a developmental pathway that can be traversed in both directions, that is, toward progression and selfhood, or toward regression and absorption in the figures of the past. Here is the divided human condition, the forward, maturational pull and the backward neurotic attraction that all of us feel to one degree or another at various times in our lives.

What occurs as the infant undergoes separation has been described as a "life-long mourning process" that triggers an endless search for replacement, for someone or something to fill the gap.[37] Every new step that we take toward autonomy holds the threat of loss. We agonize as we come to differentiate ourselves from the parent, to learn in our body-minds what separation means.[38] In this way, our very ability to conceive of objects as separate in space, an ability which underlies the scientific view of the world, is awakened early in life in close association to the dilemma of separation from the caregiver.[39] Our persistent tendency toward dualism, our curious ability to exist *in* a world that is at the same time, somehow, *out there*, is itself an expression of the manner in which we go *inward* with internalization as separation occurs and *outward* through cognitive growth. We must recall in all of this the overwhelming extent to which the limbic system, or that portion of the brain that triggers our emotional interaction with objects, is involved in mental functioning during the early time.[40] What is internalized as differentiation takes place, as the ability to represent the absent object (and hence all future objects) increases, is internalized movingly, with love and hate and fear. The so-called objective thought, or approach to creation, that comes later sits as it were on top of this primal condition and is always influenced by it. Every evolving conception of the outer universe comes into contact with and emanates from the bodily world, the world that is loaded with the frustration and desire, the longing and disappointment, that entered it during the separation phase.

7.   The Sands of Time and the Container of Space

There is virtually unanimous agreement among developmental psychologists that our sense of time or duration, which underlies perceptually everything we do, originates in the anxious stress of the mother-child relationship.[41] What is crucial for us to remember here is the tight connection between the needy infant's posture of anticipation, the change it produces in the caretaker, the resulting stimulation of the infant, and the growth of temporal awareness. I am not suggesting that the baby possesses an organized time sense. I am suggesting, rather, that immediately after his emergence from the womb innate factors become subsumed in the mother-child dialogue and hence colored by the powerful emotions that characterize that dialogue. What was biological becomes psychological, experienced in the child's developing ego as part of the link to the gradually emerging parental figure.[42]

The imperfect pattern of the child's needs and the mother's availability prompts the infant to protect himself from frustration by *anticipating* the fulfilment of his wishes. Time is subjectively experienced as separation from the nourishing object, a traumatic event, and as fantasied reunion.[43] This anticipation is closely tied to the infant's primitive, bodily awareness of change, and the awareness of change, as William James pointed out to us long ago, is the most rudimentary or primitive condition on which our sense of a time flow depends.[44]

In this way, if our perception is tied categorically to our sense of duration, and if our sense of duration is tied psychologically to motivational processes involving the caregiver, then time and the caregiver, time and the internalized object, are not merely connected at the deepest level of our being but connected in a *conflictual* way. For the infant to experience time as such it is necessary that he go through a process in which he experiences the mother as both need-fulfilling and frustrating. He is both gratified and *made to wait*, for food and for care generally.The waiting is sometimes a torment. The gratification is sometimes a blissful release. These are the foundational facts which underlie our symbolic notions of infinity--infinite woe, infinite bliss, and all the variations and nuances we encounter in the realms of ordinary and non-ordinary reality, including mathematics.[45] The atomistic time of the physicist, for example, is fashioned "above" this emotional material in what may be an effort to suppress its existence. The unconscious mental activity that is always occurring "beneath" our conscious operations has at its core a powerful intentionality--desires, feelings, aims--which cannot be dissociated from the temporal awareness that dawns with the first, ambivalent relationship.

Like time, space is closely associated with the first relationship. Indeed, psychic space comprises a kind of container which can be originally connected to the maternal caretaking function and to the absorption of infantile fantasies and fears. The capacity to experience space is a primary aspect of the ego which seems to have emerged from sensations upon the foetal skin at birth, thereby awakening the skin, with its sense receptors, into its function as a surface, as a boundary between self and non-self, and as a container of the self. Without the development of such a psychic space there can be, quite simply, no perception.[46]

The baby's non-verbalized feelings often discover their expression through the skin: it may itch, weep, rage, and so forth. Such exigencies will be dealt with by the mother according to her ability to accept and soothe the blemished infant who will, in turn, internalize the experience. The mother demonstrates how the containing figure, herself, is experienced concretely as a skin. It is precisely this function that triggers the rudimentary idea of external and internal space.[47]

With regard more specifically to the relationship between space and the differentiation phase discussed earlier, we must bear in mind that spatial representations are an integral part of the individual's attempt to understand and organize his perceptual world and to achieve differentiation. The growth of what we have called object relations occurs with progress in the separation of the self from objects and with increased articulation of the self and objects. Such advances can be evaluated by the development of spatial representations. Thus the self as we usually conceive of it needs some *place* to live and to perceive. When we speak of the "breathing room" which individuals require to maintain their existence in the world we recapitulate unconsciously the whole struggle of the human being to escape the womb that crushes and expels him at term, to cope with the appearance of the bad maternal object whose imperfect care makes him choke with rage, and to survive the loss of the good maternal figure who breathes his very life into his mouth.

The defensive strategies of the early time are formed within levels of spatial representation which are the cognitive matrix out of which defensive strategies arise. When we withdraw, we withdraw to some place, some psychic place, that allows us to withdraw there. We split the maternal figure off to another place which permits us to split it off. We reduce the world to a space in which we dwell securely, our substitute womb of enumerated types. The very notion of separateness implies exclusion, implies boundaries which establish the end of one individual and the beginning of another. When the French philosopher Gaston Bachelard reminds us that "all really inhabited space bears the essence of the notion of home,"[48] he only calls to mind the connection between spatial representation and the problem of mothering, for all notions of home bear the essence of the notion of mother.

8. The Stimulus Itself

The processes I have been describing are primarily pre-verbal ones. I want now to discuss the nature of human perception as it develops toward the symbolic phase in which internalization meets and combines with the individual's linguistic capacity. By the time this developmental phase has concluded the individual will have set up within himself a world of mental pictures and ideas which discovers its full expression in the use of the sounds we call language. However, as a bridge between the splitting of the early period and the later development of language I will concentrate briefly on another aspect of the first relationship that sheds light on the way in which the human creature comes to associate the internalized object with the whole process of bodily and emotional stimulation.

The function of mothering is largely protective. The caretaker not only avoids the dangers of the outside world, she also protects the infant from sheer over-stimulation. In fact, the management of stimulation is more or less what mothering is. I do not mean that mother simply avoids loud sounds and bright lights, for the matter goes deeper than this and bears upon the entire question of the child's growth and development. An essential feature of mothering entails the mother's ability to screen the stimuli that impinge on her child in a way that makes it possible for him to develop connections between relevant stimuli and his inner readiness to respond to them.[49] Good mothering furthers appropriate learning precisely through the screening of the stimulus field. When developmental psychologists such as Piaget remind us that stimuli are meaningful only as they fit the schema of inner processes, they call to mind another vital fact, namely that interference with the formation of connections between inner and outer events impedes development and forces the child to continue his dependence on the mother. Thus, if the caretaker fails to protect the child from overstimulation he becomes handicapped in learning to differentiate and to link outer and inner experience. Moreover, exposure to an undifferentiated stimulus (an alarm bell, for example) can make stimulation itself seem threatening. Although the mother who neglects her baby does not, at least, contribute to overstimulation, her neglect may in itself create a situation in which the environment becomes disturbing. The point is, whichever way the development takes place, the child's experience of himself and of his world is mediated through the tactual, visual, and kinesthetic contact with the mother. His initial intake of the world comes through her and with her. This passive-receptiveness in which the caretaker teaches the child to touch the world with his probing senses has been called by Erik Erikson the oldest and the most neglected mode of our experiencing.[50] What is the upshot? Clearly, that the object of the inner world in both its good and bad aspects is inextricably conjoined with our reception of stimuli in the widest sense and hence with our perception of the world in the widest sense. Our internal reactions to the stimuli that impinge upon us do not follow exclusively physiological laws. At every stage of his development the human creature is a psycho-physical entity in which bodily and emotional processes are fused.

9. The Word

Nearly half a century ago the pioneering investigations of the Russian linguist Vygotsky[51] made clear that the development of language was not primarily a cognitive process (the orthodox view) but an interactive, social process loaded with emotional, bodily components from the pre-verbal period. Because thought and speech develop in a parallel and reciprocal fashion we must ultimately think of language as a dynamic system of meaning in which the emotional and the intellectual unite. The egocentric speech of the three-year-old does not disappear when the child reaches seven or eight. Instead of atrophying,

such egocentric speech goes underground.   That is, it turns into inner
speech and forms the foundation of that inward babble which, joined to
higher cognitive components, comes eventually to comprise a sizeable
portion of our ordinary consciousness. In this way, the development of
thinking is not from the individual to the social but from the social to
the individual. The child starts conversing with himself as he has been
doing with others. As for the spoken word, it is initially a substitute for
the gesture, for the bodily attitude and bodily expression that precede
the verbalized sound. When the child says "mama" it is not merely the
word that means, say, put me in the chair, but the child's whole
behavior at that moment, his reaching out for the chair, trying to hold it,
etc. In contrast to the egocentric speech that goes inward, verbalized
speech goes outward; the child uses it as a method of pointing. It is the
fusion of this inward speech and developing outward speech that finally
comprises human thought in its ordinary, basic expression. We
appreciate from this viewpoint the growing psychological realization,
based explicitly on Vygotsky's work, that thinking is an unconscious
process in the first instance.[52]   Even our conscious speech, the
psychological community has come to recognize, is pervaded by
unconscious mechanisms to the degree that it is tied to our thinking.[53]
This means that our thinking, our stream of consciousness itself in the
most general, all-inclusive sense, is the source of those slips of the
tongue on which Freud stumbled nearly a century ago. With regard to
the role of *separation* in all of this, we must note that the *formation* of
words arises from the infant's shared experience with the mother. The
common act of referential pointing starts with the mother's invitation
but soon leads to the child inviting the mother to join in the
contemplation of some object. This marks the beginning of what
psychologists call intellectual stereoscopy in which the objectification
of the world is dependent on social interaction.[54] The child names
things *to* someone, and the loving feedback he receives becomes the
incentive for naming further things. The whole idea of two-ness and
separateness derives from this mutuality. Thus the presence and
absence of the mother and of important physical objects in the child's
world play motivational roles in the development of representational
thought. In fact, the ability to recognize mother, to conceptualize her as
mother, is goaded into existence by the need to cope with her absence,
or loss. The feeling of loss becomes the motive for acquiring the
capacity to represent absent objects or to represent objects regardless of

their presence or absence. When the baby names the absent object he predicates it on the basis of its former presence; thus, mommy gone. The same act can predicate a future presence on a current absence. The ideas of gone and mommy are linked and placed in relation to one another. The whole business of linguistic predication is thus associated with the problem of separation from the caretaker.

Again, as the child links up mommy and gone he creates a dependent relationship between two ideas that substitutes for each idea's dependency on actual experience. This gives the child the power to recall the mother at will, and the word becomes his way back to the object, the magical tie that reunites him with the "god of the nursery."[55] It is not merely that maternal stimulation during the time of language development is necessary for the fulfillment of the child's potential; our linguistic mentation is charged with the emotional energy that went into our life and death struggle to maintain our connection to the caregiver at the same time we were giving her up.[56] Through the early imperfections of mothering we learn to grip the world with our bodies, with our tense anticipation (the time sense). Through the crises of separation which continue to transpire after the early period we learn to grip the world with our minds, with our words. The mirror phase of infancy eventually gives way to the representational mirror of a mind that has separation on its mind. The very running on of our thoughts in ordinary consciousness becomes a link to the figures of the past.[57] The problem, of course, is that these figures recall not only the good side of our early existence but the bad side as well, the side that is loaded with frustration, rage, envy, anxiety, and disappointment, the side that speaks for the ambivalence of the primary years. Moreover, no matter how bad the internalized object is, the wish for reunion persists. Indeed, the internalization of particularly bad materials paradoxically increases the intensity of that wish.

10. The Tie to the Culture

The child's tendency to cope with separation through the internalizing and splitting of the object, and eventually through verbalization, culminates in his ability to create an entire symbolical universe and to have it inside himself in a space that D. W. Winnicott calls "transitional"--a term that indicates here the movement away from the caregiver and toward the wider world. In favorable circumstances, or when mothering is "good enough" to prompt ordinary development, Winnicott informs us, the child's "potential space" becomes filled with the products of his own creative imagination. If he is given the chance, the baby will begin "to live creatively and to use actual objects to be creative into." If he is not given the chance, then there is "no area in which the baby may have play," or may have cultural experience; then there is "no link with the cultural inheritance," and "no contribution to the cultural pool."[58]

Here is the process in some detail. The "good-enough mother" begins by adapting almost completely to the infant's needs. As time goes on, she adapts less and less completely according to the infant's growing ability to deal with her failure through his own experience. If all goes well, the infant can actually gain from his frustration by developing his own idiosyncratic style of relative independence. What is essential is that the mother give the baby, through her good-enough care, the "illusion" that there is "an external reality that corresponds to the infant's own capacity to create." It is precisely within this area of creativity that the infant will begin to make his transition away from the maternal figure by choosing "transitional objects"--blankets, teddy bears, story books--which afford him the magical or illusory belief *that he is moving toward, or staying with, the caretaker at the same time that he is moving away from her or giving her up.* Such magic, such illusion, such creativity provides the child with his primary link to the cultural realm, to the religious, artistic, and scientific symbols that comprise the shared, illusory reality of grown-ups. In this way, there is a "direct development" from transitional concerns to playing, and from playing to shared playing, and from this to cultural experience.[59]

On the one hand, then, our ability to make symbols, to imagine, to create, to use our powerful brains, is an innate ability that is nourished into production by maternal care. On the other hand, however, that ability is prodded into action by the very real problem of maternal separation. In the development of symbolic thought, and in the perceptual style that arises from it, there is an element of that conversion, that rooted discontentment of body and of mind, which we have been describing all along. Accordingly, there is both accuracy and profundity in Geza Roheim's contention that culture itself, at the deepest psychological level, is a way back to the parent, a symbolic connection to the early time. Thinking, says Roheim, is deeply rooted in the emotions, and between thinking and the emotions the mental image magically resides. It means *both* away from the object (separation accomplished) and back to the object (separation overcome). As a cultural item, the word links the internal and external worlds; it "summons the mother when the child is hungry." Civilization originates "in delayed infancy, and its function is security." It is a "huge network of more or less successful attempts to protect mankind against the danger of object-loss, the colossal efforts made by a baby who is afraid of being left alone in the dark."[60] While it is important to remember that language is not a system for the transmission of truth but for the creation of belief, it is equally important to bear in mind that such belief has its rooted, unconscious aspect at the center of which resides the need for the absent caregiver.

Roheim's views are strikingly supported by Eli Sagan's recent volume, *At the Dawn of Tyranny*. Maintaining that "the psyche is the paradigm for the development of culture and society," and following closely Margaret Mahler's depiction of psychic development from the symbiotic stage through the phases of separation and individuation, Sagan views the human community as a whole passing from a) early kinship organizations rooted in the familial bond, to b) complex organizations based on chieftainship and comprising the first, wrenching move *away* from kinship, to c) monarchic and archaic civilizations (Egypt, China) based upon elaborate, hierarchical arrangements which ensure individual security through stable social order. Sagan writes,

> Society may choose to resist . . . the drive toward development, but once advance is resolved upon, society is not free to take any direction . . . it wants. No primitive society develops into an archaic or classical civilization. Every primitive society that embarks on a developmental journey becomes a complex society. The logic within this advance is not primarily economic, or scientific, or even rational; . . . it is primarily a psychological logic. The stages in development from primitive to chieftainship to early monarchies to complex monarchies to archaic civilization are projections and magnifications onto

society as a whole of stages in the development of the psyche. The journey of the psyche through the various phases in the process of separation and individuation is recapitulated in social development.[61]

As for the advanced, democratic society in which we exist today, it is "the least dependant upon fundamental kinship ties of any political system ever invented."[62]

What is crucial for us to remember here is the two-sided or ambivalent character of the drive toward individuation, which endlessly struggles with the wish for the absent object. Where Roheim writes that civilization is "a huge network of attempts to protect mankind against object-loss," Sagan observes that "all forms of social cohesion are based upon kinship and are descended from kinship."[63] There is a fundamental similarity in these views. The attachment to the chief, to the Oedipal monarch, which characterizes the move from kinship to complex social organization is ultimately rooted in the tie to the internalized object of infancy and childhood. Declares Sagan, "slowly and painfully, society has been attempting over thousands of years to construct new forms of attachment and reassurance that would compensate us for our kinship paradise lost."[64] Such "forms of attachment" perforce find their way to the ground of our perception.

Thinking specifically on the methods of psychological defense discovered during the past eighty years, I would suggest that the life of ordinary consciousness is not merely a dream, as the old saying has it, but a projective dream, one that invariably projects the objects of the inner world upon the objects of the environment. We do not perceive the world subjectively--the customary claim--but objectively in the sense that includes the parental figures as the target of the infant's desires. Projection is a feature of everyday awareness, and more than that, it holds materials from the deep and conflictual past, including the separation stage. All mental presentations are actively perceptual. We meet the sense impression half way. From early infancy on, whenever we mentally attend, classify, anticipate, orient, or understand, we project.[65]

In this way, the struggle to differentiate oneself from the object is actually a struggle for what Roheim called "dual-unity,"[66] a magical condition in which one exists "on his own," separate and detached from the object, and yet, at the same time, united with the object at the unconscious, affective level. Which means, of course, that our perceptual style, our mode of ordinary consciousness, is not merely projective in a broad, preoedipal sense, but projective with specifically *transitional concerns* at the center--transitional concerns as they are defined in the work of Winnicott examined a few paragraphs earlier. Ordinary awareness is transitional awareness, a perceptive condition in which we strive to maintain our tie to the inner world by discovering substitute objects in the "reality" of our cultural realm. Needless to say, because our inward objects are both "good" and "bad" in their deeply internalized aspects much of our substitutive seeking reveals a negative or destructive intent. Our dual-unity is established through the suffering and sacrifice of others, or through the defeatist, self-inimical treatment of ourselves. In the second part of this volume we will take this matter up in some detail. And in the third and final part, we will discuss the possibility of achieving an awareness that is less obsessively transitional in nature than the one we currently employ.

11. The Oedipus, and After

Internalization of stress does not cease with the close of the primary years. On the contrary, the neonate emerges from this turbulent period to confront the strain of the Oedipal phase during which the emotional and sensual desire for the parent of the opposite sex creates a fear of castration in the male child (we will come to the female in a moment), as well as powerful feelings of ambivalence and jealousy toward the male parent.

This is a time of great anxiety for the boy whose dilemma will be imperfectly and paradoxically resolved through identification with the father. That is to say, perceiving the hopelessness of removing his rival, the child begins to identify with him (identification, remember, is a form of internalization) and to strive and compete in the male world of which the father is the chief representative. As his wounded narcissism benefits from his boyish accomplishments and interactions, he gradually adopts the male point of view. Typically, his wishes and aims are now bound up with heroic achievements, glory, domination; yet the wish for the mother persists at the deepest levels, and a conflicted dependency on the father develops as a refuge from separation and loss.

The entire syndrome finds its expression in romantic and/or

authoritarian fantasies and behaviors. As males, we go through life longing for the perfect woman (which means for mother), fearing emasculation at the hands of both women and men, identifying with symbols of power and control (the nation, the leader, the company, the winning team, wealth), and making the best of what we perceive to be our failures and shortcomings. It is a pathetic picture, and would even be ridiculous were it not so replete with deep and genuine discontentment. When the Buddha thousands of years ago bluntly maintained that life is suffering he probably had some ancient version of this syndrome in mind. For us, the Buddha's insight may be bluntly restated: all life that remains emotionally and perceptually tied to the internalizations of the primary years is fated to be neurotic and stressful.

For the female child the dynamics of the Oedipal phase are rather different; the stress that results, however, can be just as intense. If a single utterance had to be made to get at the essentials of the matter it would point out that the girl's partial absorption (as opposed to the boy's almost total absorption) into the father's socially oriented universe during the resolution of the Oedipal crisis leaves the female child more directly and uninterruptedly in the midst of the pre-Oedipal, maternally centered issues which characterize the first years of life. Hence the girl is more prone than the boy to evince open, on-going concern with boundary issues, or issues of separation and merger, and to regard the male parent (and his later substitutes) not so much as an avenue away from the mother's world as a means of resolving problems inextricably tied to the imperfections of the mother's care. In even briefer compass, girls (and women) remain absorbed in the issue of closeness, and when girls (and women) discover themselves involved with normal males who fear such closeness, whose lives have been directed away from precisely such closeness, the old, familiar tension between the sexes results, adding yet another strain to people's ordinary lives.

Several years after the close of the Oedipal period, adolescence brings forth its weighty issues: genital sexuality, increasing separation from the parental presence, the forging of a consistent, integrated character, and a growing awareness of adult imperfections. It is a formidable list, and for millions, a hellish time, exacerbated today by a decline of familial support and cohesion, by a world of impersonal technological forces and influences, by an increasingly unhealthful, polluted environment (adult failure at the stewardship of the planet), and by the annihilative, "doomsday" weaponry of the world's "great powers."

Of course neither Oedipal nor adolescent issues are strictly *perceptual* ones, as the issues of the mirror and separation stages are. By the age of six, and obviously by the age of twelve or thirteen, the perceptual apparatus in its underlying, unconscious essentials is complete. Indeed, the Oedipal period and adolescence characteristically inherit, and are shaped by, the problems and forces of the foundational years.[67] And that is the point. The stress of the later dilemmas deepens the primal, mind-body *conversion* that we have been describing. Our projective, transitional style of perceiving the world is considerably intensified as Oedipal and adolescent struggles absorb the anxiety and splitting of the early time.

Notes and References
Part One

1. For a solid discussion of projective identification see Kernberg, Otto F. "Projection and Projective Identification." *Journal of the American Psychoanalytic Association,* 35 (1987), 795-819.
2. Freud, Sigmund. "The Defence Neuro-Psychoses." [1894] In *Collected Papers,* ed. Joan Riviere. New York: Basic Books, 1959, Vol. 1, p. 63.
3. See Mushatt, Cecil. "Mind Body Environment." *Psychoanalytic Quarterly,* 44 (1975), 84-107.
4. Freud, Sigmund. "Further Remarks on the Defence Neuro-Psychoses." [1896] In *Collected Papers,* ed. cit., p. 163.
5. de Mause, Lloyd. *Foundations of Psychohistory.* New York: Creative Roots, Inc., 1982.
6. Greenspan, Stanley I. *First Feelings: Milestones in the Development of Your Baby and Child.* New York: Viking Books, 1985.
7. Kail, Robert. *The Development of Memory in Children.* New York: W. H. Freeman, 1984, p. 115.
8. *Ibid.,* p. 129.
9. Almansi, Renato J. "On the Persistence of Very Early Memory Traces in Psychoanalysis." *Journal of the American Psychoanalytic Association,* 31 (1983), 391-421.
10. Delgado, Jose. *Physical Control of the Mind.* New York: Harper and Row, 1971, p. 26.
11. I am indebted here to the writings of Joseph C. Rheingold, and in particular to his *Fear of Being a Woman,* New York: Grune and Stratton, 1964.
12. The manner in which the caretaker shapes the infant's budding ego is brought out particularly well in Stern, Daniel. "The Early Development of Schemes of Self, Other, and Self With Other." In *Reflections on Self Psychology,* ed. Joseph D. Lichtenberg and Samuel Kaplan. Hillsdale, New Jersey: The Analytic Press, 1983, pp. 49-84.
13. Menaker, Esther. "A Kohut Symposium." *Psychoanalytic Review,* 65 (1978), 621.
14. See McCall, Robert B. *Infants.* New York: Vintage Books, 1979.
15. Spitz, Rene. *The First Year of Life.* New York: International Universities Press, 1965, p. 81.
16. Gaddini, Eugenio. "Notes on the Mind-Body Question." *International Journal of Psychoanalysis,* 68 (1987), 315-329.

17. I am indebted here and in the following paragraph to H. M. Southwood's, "The Origin of Self-Awareness and Ego Behavior," *International Journal of Psychoanalysis*, 54 (1973), 235-239.
18. Winnicott, D. W. *Playing and Reality*. London: Penguin Books, 1971, p. 130.
19. Stern, Daniel. *The First Relationship: Mother and Infant*. Cambridge, Mass.: Harvard University Press, 1977.
20. See Beres, David. "Perception, Imagination, and Reality." *International Journal of Psychoanalysis*, 41 (1960), 327-334.
21. See Rank, Otto. *The Trauma of Birth*. London: Kegan-Paul, 1929.
22. See Mahler, Margaret S., Pine, Fred, and Bergman, Anni. *The Psychological Birth of the Human Infant*. New York: Basic Books, 1975, p. 227.
23. Eigen, Michael."Toward Bion's Starting Point: Between Catastrophe and Fate." *International Journal of Psychoanalysis*, 66 (1985), 329.
24. See Rheingold's, *The Fear of Being a Woman*, ed. cit., p. 164.
25. Schiffer, Irvine. *The Trauma of Time*. New York: International Universities Press, 1979.
26. See Schultz, Clarence G. "The Struggle Toward Ambivalence." *Psychiatry*, 47 (1984), 28-36.
27. Lax, Ruth. "The Role of Internalization in the Development of Female Masochism." *International Journal of Psychoanalysis*, 58 (1977), 289-300.
28. Broucek, Francis. "Efficacy in Infancy." *International Journal of Psychoanalysis*, 60 (1979), 311-316.
29. Meares, Russell. "On the Ownership of Thought." *Psychiatry*, 49 (1986), 80-95.
30. Bloch, Dorothy. *So the Witch Won't Eat Me*. New York: Harper and Row, 1979.
31. Neumann, Erich. *The Great Mother*. Princeton: Princeton University Press, 1970, p. 148.
32. Once again I am indebted to Rheingold's, *The Fear of Being a Woman*, ed. cit., p. 148.
33. Steinzor, Bernard. "Death and the Construction of Reality." *Omega: Journal of Death and Dying*, 9 (1979), 97-124.
34. Stein, Howard. *Developmental Time, Cultural Space*. Norman: University of Oklahoma Press, 1987, p. 189.
35. Coen, Stanley J. "Notes on the Concepts of Self object and Pre-Oedipal Self object." *Journal of the American Psychoanalytic Association*, 29 (1981), 395-411.
36. I am indebted here and in the following sentences to Fred Pines' "On the Pathology of the Separation-Individuation Crisis." *International*

Journal of Psychoanalysis, 60 (1979), 225-242.

37 . See Rizzuto, Ana-Maria. *The Birth of the Living God.* Chicago: University of Chicago Press, 1979, p. 49.

38 . Slipp, Samuel. *Object Relations: A Dynamic Bridge Between Individual and Family Treatment.* New York: Jason Aronson, 1984, p. 52.

39 . See Akhundov, Murad D. *Conceptions of Space and Time,* trans. Charles Rougle. Cambridge, Mass.: MIT Press, 1986, pp. 4-5.

40 . Taylor, Gordon R. *The Natural History of the Mind.* London: Granada Books, p. 110.

41 . See Hartocollis, Peter. "Origins of Time." *Psychoanalytic Quarterly,* 43(1974), pp. 243-261.

42 . See Colarusso, Calvin. "The Development of the Time Sense." *International Journal of Psychoanalysis,* 60 (1979), 243-252.

43 . Arlow, Jacob. "Disturbances of the Sense of Time." *Psychoanalytic Quarterly,* 53 (1984), 15.

44 . James, William. *Principles of Psychology.* New York: Henry Holt, 1890, Vol. 1, p. 62.

45 . See Grosholz, Emily. "A New View of Mathematical Knowledge." *British Journal of the Philosophy of Science,* 36 (1985), 71-78.

46 . Grotstein, James. "Inner Space: Its Dimensions and Coordinates." *International Journal of Psychoanalysis,* 59 (1978), 53-61.

47 . Pines, Dinora. "Skin Communication." *International Journal of Psychoanalysis,* 61 (1980), 315-324.

48. Bachelard, Gaston. *The Poetics of Space.* Boston: Beacon, 1969, p.5.

49. I am indebted here to Arno Gruen, "The Discontinuity in the Ontogeny of the Self." *Psychoanalytic Review,* 61 (1974), 557-569.

50. Erikson, Eric H. *Young Man Luther,* New York: Norton, 1958,p. 208.

51. Vygotsky, L. S. *Thought and Language* [1934]. Cambridge, Mass.: MIT Press, 1979, pp. 30-40.

52. See Basch, Michael. "Psychoanalytic Interpretation and Cognitive Transformation." *International Journal of Psychoanalysis,* 62 (1981), 151-174.

53. Roustang, Francois. *Dire Mastery: Discipleship from Freud to Lacan.* Baltimore: Johns Hopkins University Press, 1976, p. 63.

54. I am indebted in this and the following paragraph to David Bleich's, "New Considerations of the Infantile Acquisition of Language and Symbolic Thought." Presented to the *Psychological Center for the Study of the Arts,* Buffalo, New York, 1970, pp. 1-28.

55. Shengold, Leonard. "The Effects of Child Abuse: George Orwell." *Psychoanalytic Quarterly,* 54 (1985), 26.

56. Bady, Susan Lee. "The Voice as a Curative Factor in Psychotherapy." *Psychoanalytic Review,* 72 (1985), 479-490.

57. Andresen, Jeffrey. "Why People Talk to Themselves." *Journal of*

the American Psychoanalytic Association, 28 (1980), 449-518.
    58. Winnicott, D. W. "The Location of Cultural Experience."
International Journal of Psychoanalysis, 48 (1966), 368-372.
    59. Winnicott, D. W. *Playing and Reality*. London: Penguin Books,
1971, p. 12.
    60. Roheim, Geza. *The Origin and Function of Culture*. New York:
Doubleday and Co., 1971, p. 131.
    61. Sagan, Eli. *At the Dawn of Tyranny*. New York: Alfred A. Knopf,
1985, p. 364.
    62. *Ibid.*, p. 375.
    63. *Ibid.*, p. 371.
    64. *Ibid.*, p. 222.
    65. See Ornston, Darius. "On Projection." *The Psychoanalytic Study of
the Child*. New Haven: Yale University Press, 1978, Vol. 33, pp. 117-166.
    66. Roheim, Geza. *Magic and Schizophrenia*. Bloomington: Indiana
University Press, 1962.
    67. Dorpat, Theodore L. "Man and Mind: Collected Papers of Jeanne
Lampl-De Groot." *Seattle Institute for Psychoanalysis Newsletter*, 2 (1988), 4-5.
Dorpat quotes Lampl-De Groot as follows: "Little by little I became aware of
the immanent importance of the early preoedipal mother-child relationship for
the shaping of the oedipal situation" (p. 4).

Part Two

The Cultural Sphere

1. Some Background

Psychoanalytic investigations of culture have been hampered by their failure to begin at the beginning, to address the problem of civilization and its discontents *after* having probed the manner in which our ordinary consciousness comes about. All the psychoanalytic studies of culture conducted in the grand manner--and I am thinking here primarily on the work of Freud, Reich, Brown, Marcuse, Roheim, and Becker--are written as if our world of ordinary awareness were somehow *given* rather than *made*. Although the writers just mentioned are supremely appreciative of the manner in which neurosis matures and, as it were, expands toward the cultural realm which then comes to influence the individual born into it (let's not get involved in a chicken-egg debate, yet), they do not see that ordinary consciousness, the psychological universe *in which* neurosis comes to work, is itself a psychological problem, a condition of tension and stress which powerfully determines the nature of our institutions.

To express it somewhat differently, psychoanalytic investigations of culture are philosophically naive to the extent that they assume ordinary consciousness is not, itself, a subject of analysis. Such investigations require a phenomenological slant, a willingness to uncover the very origins of awareness, to grasp the ways in which awareness takes shape, *and then* to proceed to the manner in which specific "drives" are moulded by the cultural forces the individual inherits. As it turns out, the failure to explore ordinary consciousness as a preliminary to the study of culture has had the effect of leaving the worm unperceived in the bud; for the essence of mankind's dilemma is bound up inextricably with the development not of its neurosis as we usually conceive of that but with the development of its "normal" mentation, the *ground* in which neurosis takes root.

Obviously I do not have the space in this relatively brief work to deal at length with each of the major theoreticians just cited. Therefore, I will offer a few representative examples which underscore my thesis and which adumbrate the nature of the discussion to follow, and I will use the occasional footnote to fill in the gaps and complete the picture

29

in an incisive, economical way.

Freud writes in *The Future of an Illusion* that "scientific work" and "scientific observation" are the best foundation for examining "external reality."[1] On another page of the same book he contends that "religion consists of certain dogmas, assertions about the facts and conditions of external and internal reality."[2] With no disrespect to Freud, this actually calls to mind Piaget's observation that children "gradually construct" the "universe" around them and then go on to experience that universe as "external to themselves," as something that is really *there*, thus making it difficult for themselves as grownups to realize that their entire "psychological evolution" was determined by the nature of their early development, their first constructions of space and time.[3]

But the truly crucial passage occurs toward the close of this work where Freud writes of our "mental apparatus" as follows:

> Firstly, it has been developed actually in the attempt to explore the outer world, and therefore it must have realized in its structure a certain measure of appropriateness; secondly, it itself is a constituent part of that world which we investigate, and readily admits of such investigation; thirdly, the task of science is fully circumscribed if we confine it to showing how the world must appear to us in consequence of the particular character of our organization.[4]

The development of ordinary awareness, then, is of little interest to psychoanalysis. Our ordinary consciousness, our mental "organization," must be more or less as nature intended it to be or else we would have encountered difficulty in exploring the world. The fact that such exploration culminated ultimately in the neurotic, illusory condition of mankind in culture (Freud's persistent theme here), is apparently forgotten for the moment. Indeed, had Freud concluded that our "organization" in its development and application seemed suspect in terms of what we have become as a species, had he suggested that the sick animal's sickness might have something to do with his ordinary way of perceiving the universe, he would have reached a conclusion more in keeping with the context of *The Future of an Illusion* and the substance of his later work, *Civilization and Its Discontents*. There is surely very little "appropriateness" in the picture of man which emerges from these books.

The philosophical limitations of Brown's *Life Against Death* emerge early when he writes that the "crux of Freud's discovery is that neurotic symptoms, as well as the dreams and errors of everyday life, do have meaning, and that the meaning of 'meaning' has to be radically revised" because of this. He then declares, "since the purport of these purposive expressions is generally unknown to the person whose purpose they express, Freud is driven to embrace the paradox that there are in a human being purposes of which he knows nothing, involuntary purposes, or unconscious ideas."[5] What needs to be stressed immediately is that our ordinary consciousness, our ordinary way of perceiving and being in the world, is itself one of these unconscious ideas, is itself an involuntary response to the pressures and anxieties of experience, a defensive, transitional gripping of "reality" commenced during the preoedipal period and employed as a tie to the relinquished object. As we have seen, the child's perception is the mother's perception. Surely Freud's monumental discovery that, in the words of Brown, "neurosis is not just an occasional aberration; it is in us, and in us all the time,"[6] must, on the face of it, bear a crucial relation to the origins of our everyday awareness, the awareness that constitutes quite as much a part of people's mental life as do their dreams and slips of the tongue. It is the *whole mind* that is neglected in the analysis, and it is "normal" waking consciousness, apart from its slips, which escapes dissection precisely because it seems so normal, so natural, so "appropriate" in Freud's expression, to those who reside within it.

Intent upon questioning the "origin and legitimacy" of the environment in which we discover ourselves, Marcuse in his *Eros and Civilization* stresses Freud's philosophical importance, for like those who stand in the great traditions of philosophy, Freud strove to fashion a "theory of man," a "psychology" in the "strict sense."[7] This emphasis on philosophy is valuable as it helps us to focus the integral connection between psychological and philosophical inquiry. Yet Marcuse, for all his familiarity with phenomenological issues as they emerge in the work of Hegel and Marx, has nothing to say about the development of ordinary awareness, as "strict" an aspect of "man" as one could wish. Like Freud and Freud's followers, he writes of the "reality principle" as if that were not a subject for psychological *and philosophical* investigation. One of his paragraphs begins, "with the establishment of the reality principle," and proceeds to declare that "under the reality principle" people develop the "function of reason" and learn to "test the reality."[8] But it is precisely what is happening to and with the individual as this "reality" enters the picture during the preoedipal phase that comprises the ground of our understanding of what happens to the individual after the "reality" has "established" itself. Unless the origins of awareness are meticulously explored in exactly this regard, what *is* happening as "reality" arises will never be clear. True, Marcuse has a fine sense of how political and economic regimes foster the "reality" in which citizens exist; he knows that political and economic "realities" are relative to eras and ideologies. This does not obviate the need, however, to examine the roots of human perception, for it is *from* those roots that ideologies and eras derive.

Ernest Becker asserts in his *Denial of Death* that "what bothers people is incongruity, life as it *is*."[9] We have here an instance of Becker's belief that human beings choose to exist in an illusory, symbolic universe that shields them from the raw truths of meaninglessness and death. Life in the symbolic mode is not what *is*. There *is* a "reality," however, presumably some sort of objective one, that people are afraid of seeing, for in order to see it, they must leave their "symbolic world," the world in which "everything they do" is an attempt "to deny" the "grotesqueness" of "their fate."[10] Yet is not the world that people will "see" *after* they have abandoned their symbolic activities also a world that is explicitly perceived through a symbolic channel? There is not *one word* in *The Denial of Death* or in the later *Escape from Evil* about the nature of perception *out of* the symbolic framework, let alone about the methods required to *get* out of it. (This will become a central issue in the final pages of our discussion.) To advance what *is* as opposed to what is "illusory," to postulate a realm of "empirical truth,"[11] merely returns us to the old dualistic position adopted by Freud in his book on "illusion," with "objectivity" over here and "subjectivity" over there. It will not do, for it fails to appreciate the extent to which realities--*all* realities--are *made* by the individuals who inhabit them. Realities stand in *some* sort of integral relation to ordinary consciousness, itself a *perceptual state* in which the internalized object projectively governs the functioning of our "mental apparatus" and hence the nature of our questing in culture.

Psychoanalytic investigations of culture have evinced another shortcoming which limits severely their contribution to our understanding of civilized society, namely their failure to explore the implications--and I include here the economic implications--of the mother-infant bond, particularly with reference to internalization and splitting. As we have seen, ordinary awareness has a crucial defensive purpose: it provides the individual with a psychological avenue back to the mothering figure. The symbolic contents of the human mind, or the "stuff" of ordinary reality, get there in the main through our biological ability to internalize the world. And as the internalization of the maternal object is the chief defensive maneuver of the helpless, dependent, anxious human infant, the symbolic proclivity of people comes to be automatically associated with the need to retain, to hold on to, the mother. We do not merely perceive the world with our minds; we grip it. Man is not simply the "symbol-making animal" who lives in a world "apart from nature," as hundreds of modern scholars are fond of maintaining. He is the animal who uses his symbols *defensively, projectively* to answer the crises of his intrapsychic and interpersonal life, especially those crises surrounding his separation from the parent.

Accordingly, we would expect the world of culture, which is grounded in shared awareness, in internalized attitudes and beliefs, to provide a similar security, a similar psychological avenue back to the mothering figure, a similar defensive purpose at the level of group as opposed to individual behavior. As we have also seen, Roheim got at this in a general way when he wrote that "civilization's function is security," that it provides "substitute objects" for the "baby who is afraid of being left alone in the dark"--in other words, for us.[12] Yet even Roheim's contribution must be seen as one that falls short of the mark. His conclusions were reached at the end of a long career spent in the service of Freud's Oedipal theory and are therefore streaked with the limitations of that theory. The substitute objects of culture, he declared, have ultimately a libidinal, sexual purpose. The baby who is "afraid of the dark" wants to merge incestuously with the parent.[13] In my view and in the light of major developments in psychoanalytic psychology, the nature of the infant's interaction with the mother, and hence the purpose of cultural objects, is missed, or better confused, by such an emphasis. Again, Roheim's conclusions were derived almost exclusively from his observations of primitive peoples and *never applied in a rigorous way to his own--and our--society.* This is of the utmost importance and brings me to one of my chief purposes, namely to examine *specific ways* in which culture, *including our own*, develops out of the need to retain the tie to the internalized caregiver.

Perhaps the most remarkable passage in *Civilization and Its Discontents*, the fountainhead of analytic investigations of culture, is the one in which Freud declares that religious needs are ultimately derived from the "infant's helplessness"and from the "longing for the father" which is "aroused" by such helplessness. To Freud, this causal scheme appears "incontrovertible," for he "cannot think of any need in childhood as strong as the need for a father's protection."[14] Where, one wonders immediately, is the mother in all of this, and where are those feelings bound up with the child's interaction with the mother? Is not the need for symbiosis, for union, for a close, protective relationship with the mothering figure as strong as the need for "a father's protection," and is not the problem of separation from the parents, and particularly from the mother, one of, if not *the*, central problems of childhood? It is almost astonishing that Freud could so neglect this aspect of human development in his analysis of the origin of religious needs, and, ultimately, of the cultural configurations which arise therefrom.

But the matter does not end here. For immediately after writing that the origin of the religious attitude can be traced back to the infant's feeling of helplessness and in his longing for a father's protection, Freud declares, "there may be something further behind that, but for the present it is wrapped in obscurity."[15] It is as if he senses here precisely what Otto Rank was sensing during the course of his career, and what great numbers of Freud's followers came to sense during the past five decades, namely that behind the longing for the father's protection is the longing for union with the mothering figure and the anxiety which attends the separation from her. My own feeling is that Freud resisted analysis of the mother-infant relationship throughout his life, that such resistance gave rise to psychoanalysis' most glaring theoretical weaknesses (this has been largely corrected, *except* in the area of "civilization and its discontents"), and that the sentence of Freud just cited about "something lying further behind" the helplessness of the infant and the concomitant need for the father's protection arose from Freud's scientific conscience where he knew his analysis was incomplete. The significance of the mother-infant relationship and its role in "civilization" is wrapped in obscurity in Freud's book because Freud was unwilling to unwrap it and look in.

"Freud, with his genius and his humanity," writes Brown in *Life Against Death*, "tried to keep in the field of psychoanalytical consciousness not only the problems of the neurotic patient, but also the problems of mankind as a whole." But Freud "never faced fully" the "existential and theoretical consequences" of taking on the problem of mankind's "general neurosis." He was "unable to make the shift to an anthropological point of view." What is needed is a "synthesis of psychoanalysis, anthropology, and history."[16] Yet Brown, in his own analysis, and after singling out Roheim's work as the great pioneering effort in the attempt to disclose mankind's neurosis, "second only to Freud's," chooses *not to explore Roheim's conclusion*, the upshot of everything Roheim wrote. It is not the mother-child situation that is investigated in Brown, but the vicissitudes of anality, and this along the lines of Freud's classical libido theory.

At one point Brown declares in the most forceful way that an analysis of the maternal influence is crucial to our understanding of mankind's neurosis. He even goes on to suggest that Freud's emphasis upon the father is an impediment to our progress because it prevents us from reaching the matriarchal level which lies beneath the patriarchal scheme of things. "The proper starting point for a Freudian anthropology," he writes, "is the pre-Oedipal mother. What is given by nature, in the family, is the dependence of the child on the mother. Male domination [is] a secondary formation, the product of the child's revolt against the primal mother."[17] The accuracy of these remarks seems incontestable to me; yet, in the face of them, one is struck by Brown's subsequent position. That is, on a later page, and at the heart of his discussion of economic institutions which express the sickness of man and virtually consign those born into them to a certain degree of twistedness, in other words, *our* economic institutions, he states that "identification with the father" is only a way of "denying dependence on the mother," and that "as long as psychoanalytical theory of the pre-Oedipal mother remains backward" the "individualism" of the Protestant era, and ultimately of our time, as well as the significance of the entire shift in western social organization from matriarchy to patriarchy, will "remain psychologically obscure."[18] What Brown is confessing here is this: just as Freud was not "fully equipped" to "make the shift" to an "anthropological point of view" which would have allowed him to spy a cure for mankind's "general neurosis," so Brown, in his reliance on a "backward" psychoanalytical theory, is also not fully equipped to analyse the problem to which he addresses himself in his book. For as Brown himself states, it is the mother-infant interaction which demands exploration and it is precisely that interaction which Brown doesn't explore, beyond suggesting that the problems of ambivalence and guilt, for Freud the central problems in the development of culture, have as much to do with the mother as with the father.[19] In the main, he is content with stating generally the incompleteness of the psychoanalytical theory, an incompleteness which derives from the reliance upon the father as the starting point. In short, Brown does not get very far beyond Roheim, not simply with regard to a general recognition of the mother's key role, but even with regard to his analyses of anality, wealth, repression, the unconscious, and the death drive, all of which call to mind specific observations scattered throughout the endless forests of Roheim's paragraphs.

Exploration must begin precisely where Brown says it must, and one regrets that Brown, with his enormous powers, did not choose to begin it there, for by 1959, the year in which his book appeared, writers such as Spitz, Jacobson, Winnicott, Mahler, Klein, and Fairbairn were shedding considerable and valuable light upon precisely those problems which Brown spies as crucial: the psychoanalytic nature of the first years of life, the tensions of maternal separation, and the ambivalence inherent in the mother-infant relationship. Brown's work is literally void of reference to these writers. His theory is grounded in Freud, and in those of Freud's followers who subscribed to the libido theory (Ferenczi and Abraham). Glover on Klein is about as close as he comes to the area, and even later, in *Love's Body*, he seems to have gotten around only to Klein.[20]

Eros and Civilization is also without reference to the authors just cited. From a theoretical angle Marcuse's emphasis is overwhelmingly Freudian, and his analysis of "civilization" is primarily a philosophical and sociological deepening of Freud's doctrine of repression. For Marcuse the "death instinct" or the "Nirvana principle" becomes the tendency of the individual to withdraw from a repressive society, to detach himself from an order that frustrates his instinctual life. Only in the context in which it manifests itself *socially* can the "drive" for death, for quiescence, be correctly understood. Although Marcuse, like Brown, differentiates himself from Freud by according the matriarchal, and the maternal, a fundamental significance in the development of western society,[21] he at no point *analyzes* the mother-infant interaction as relevant to the natures of those social forces which coerce the individual in the form of institutions. Not only is the discussion of these matriarchal matters too general to be genuinely innovative, it is also reflective of Freud's classical approach. The mother in *Eros and Civilization* is chiefly the "Oedipal object" of the child's sexuality, the one from whom he is separated by the father, and thus a kind of "aim-inhibitor." The "strongest of all childhood wishes" derives from the "Oedipus situation," not from anything pre-oedipal, and it is this situation to which Marcuse addresses himself as he searches for solutions to the Freudian-capitalist dilemma.[22]

Like Marcuse, Reich proffers the matriarchal as an alternative to a father dominated, phallic-dominated capitalistic order, and like Marcuse he spies in the union of Freud and Marx the ideational source of mankind's liberation.[23] Focusing intensively upon the internalization of patriarchal attitudes in the home, and maintaining that such internalization is the seedbed of fascism, Reich views people generally as trapped within their "armor," their repressed and repressive "characters" which choke off the healthful expression of their sexual instincts. But also like Marcuse, he fails to examine the mother-infant bond and hence misses the other side of the maternal realm, the side that holds the anxiety and ambivalence of the early period, the side that reflects the *bad* as well as the good object, the side that makes matriarchy as problematical as patriarchy, only for a variety of different reasons. Reich's analysis of character is, of course, brilliant, original, and a permanent contribution to psychoanalysis. I wish to stress, however, that it can obscure the extent to which the human creature is confined not merely within his sexually repressed personality but within his *perceptually crippled ordinary awareness as a whole*. People *use* their sexuality to cope with, to overcome, the preoedipal anxieties and terrors which entered their "characters" during life's first years. In this way, our sexuality becomes part of our *transitional* style of existing in the world. It is not merely our sexual nature that requires liberation; it is our entire perceiving organism that requires it.

The work of Freud, Reich, Marcuse, Brown, Roheim, and Becker comprises what we can think of as the first great wave of the psychoanalytic assault on the discontents of civilization. The second wave is currently gathering momentum with such books as Howard Stein's *Developmental Time, Cultural Space*,[24] and Eli Sagan's *At the Dawn of Tyranny*,[25] both of which we made use of in part one. The decisive influence of the preoedipal period is not merely recognized in these writings, it is applied to specific cultural configurations. More particularly, Stein examines the ways in which early anxiety and splitting govern our perceptions of geo-political space and contribute powerfully to dichotomous views of the world and resulting international tensions. Sagan traces the stress of the separation-individuation phase through a variety of social orders in an effort to disclose the manner in which the disruption of the symbiotic tie and the ambivalent pursuit of autonomy determine the nature of organizational institutions, from kinship, to monarchy, to democracy. These are important volumes and can be regarded as adjunctive to and supportive of the ideas I will put forth in the following pages. Yet once again, neither Stein nor Sagan recognizes in ordinary consciousness, in the normative reception of stimuli generally, in the normative processing of information in the widest sense, the chief source of our struggles on the planet. Neither sees in ordinary, everyday awareness the projection of infancy's transitional dilemma. Stein writes in one place that culture is ultimately an "out-of-awareness system" based upon transference relations.[26] But the most urgent point to remember in this regard is that our defensive, projective style of perceiving the world, *our ordinary consciousness itself*, is an out-of-awareness system. This is, I grant you, a startling and radical notion, yet it must be faced and worked through. Our whole perceptual-psychological style of being-in-the-world is linked to an unconscious transitional purpose and dictates the endless expression of our obsessional, mad behaviors in culture.

2. The Religio-Economic Realm

Silvio Gesell declares in his classic study *The Natural Economic Order* that "goods, not money, are the real foundation of economic life;" he then asserts, "money is a means of *exchange* and nothing else."[27] This is a crucial assertion, one that can help us to grasp what might be termed the transitional mode of economic organization, and even the transitional mode of cultural organization as a whole.

Of the transitional object itself Greenacre writes,

> It represents not only the mother's breast and body but the total maternal environment as it is experienced in combination with sensations from the infant's body. It serves as a support and 'convoy' during the period of rapid growth which necessitates increasing separation from

the mother . . . It is a protective escort. Its softness and pliability [if it happens to be a blanket, cloth etc.] are useful at a time when the infant's perceptions of the outer world are changing and when speech is forming. . . Thus it lends itself to symbolic representation and plays a role in promoting illusion by relating new experiences to earlier ones. It consolidates the illusion of maternal supplementation.[28]

What must be stressed immediately is this: the creation and use of the transitional object derives *from the same psychological impetus which lies behind the formation of symbols generally*, that is, the driving need to internalize the environment, to grip the external world and thus to answer the problem of separation with the magic of dual-unity, or the condition of having the object in fantasy and relinquishing it in "reality." Now, when we recognize that money is a powerful, complex *symbol*, that it is valued, in the words of Furnham and Lewis, "because it represents or is associated with various desirable objects,"[29] we also recognize that the *exchange* which money is fated to accomplish at the unconscious level will engage the entire separation-individuation problem. Where money is concerned "exchange" will focus directly the tension of the physical and psychological *boundaries* established by individuals and institutions, the whole "business" of "merging," "withdrawing," "taking-over," the metaphors of the marketplace in all their underlying significance. Indeed, to "exchange" is to touch upon the very basis of human existence itself, in which Eros draws forth the sexual response between people during nature's essential "transaction," one that leads to the exchange between the mother and the infant at her breast. To say that money is a means of "exchange" and "nothing else" is not simply true, it is *profoundly* true, true in a way that directs attention to the deep, affective life of the species. As for the *transitional* implications, they are clear enough: money is a transitional object triggering transitional aims; its complex symbolism reaches down to crucial issues bound up with the crises of the early period, the crises which color all subsequent psychological experience.

That money is customarily associated with *food*, with *survival*, also harbors unconscious significance and touches upon the problems of union and separation--the *oral* problems which are forever tied to the maternal object and the breast. It is in the infant's relationship with the mother that psychoanalysis spies the origin of the "oceanic feeling,"[30] the feeling in which the *boundaries* between self and other disappear, the feeling in which one exchanges himself for the other, or is indistinguishable from the other. That money is exchanged for food, is in a sense indistinguishable from food, not only links economics to psychology, particularly with regard to the mother-infant interaction, it also links economics and psychology to *religion*, and especially to religious "mysteries" in which ego boundaries disappear in the divine *exchange* between the individual and the God who is his sustenance, his food, his *wafer*. We are not dealing here simply in metaphor but in a metaphoric version of psychic reality. The "oceanic feeling" is grounded in the same bond in which religious feeling is grounded, the bond that overcomes separation.

Religion strives to answer the discontents of anxiety, separation, isolation, and mortality through its particular method of reconstituting the parental tie. However, such discontents are also addressed and paradoxically deepened by the economic system (religion's ancient adversary) which works to compensate for the original loss of the object through *substitutes*--wealth, power, possession. In the development of Protestantism the two, economics and religion, formed a joint assault on the infantile dilemma, an assault which constituted, at another level, a remarkable attempt to resolve the ancient conflict between God and gold. That conflict was not resolved, of course, because--and this is the point--the enemies, God and gold, are not really enemies at all but "brothers under the skin." As Becker reminds us in *Escape from Evil*, the power of God has always been present in the metal,[31] direct support for which may be found in the *Upanishads* (and countless other works) where the face of God is concealed behind a circle of gold.[32] The psychological meaning of all this is further expressed in religious ornament and, most strikingly, in the Protestant attempt to *deny* the equivalency by stripping the churches, an attempt that was guiltily rooted in the lust for gold which characterized Protestant life. We begin to spy from this perspective the compulsive or obsessional ground of our economic organization, the discontent of our civilization from an economic angle. Proffering a version of the maternal object, promising a magical reunion with the breast, the economic order teases, even titillates, the unconscious requirements of millions of human beings, for the desired symbiosis is *actually over*; the longed-for mother is no longer *there*. In Freud's way of looking at it, because the "gold" *itself* is *not* an infantile wish, its possession cannot bring happiness.[33] In the deepest psychoanalytic sense, then, ordinary religion and ordinary economics are *one*. Money and the sacred meet in the need to retain the tie to the object, in the dynamics of internalization and its subsequent projective creations. Not without transitional significance is the anthropologists' discovery that the first banks were temples, temples in which sanctified food was stored.[34]

3. Money and the Magna Mater

Money's *oral* significance, its unconscious connection to the objects of the early period, has of late been disclosed in a psychoanalytic literature that for decades had been ruled by theories based on the "anal stage." The sacrificial bull, William Desmonde informs us, was "often regarded as a fertility spirit or embodiment of the crops emanating from the goddess Earth." Eating the bull "represented an eating of the goddess or mother image" and expressed a wish "to incorporate the mother," to recapture the "infantile state of nondifferentiation." It was the "acquisition of money" that admitted the bearer to the sacrificial feasts and that came to signify the discovery of a "mother substitute which provided an infallible source of emotional security." Money, declares Desmonde, "originated in the obtaining and distributing of food, . . . symbolized mother's milk," and sparked "ideas and emotions connected to the breast." As for "participation in the communion symbolized by the early monetary forms," it denoted the "psychic attaining of identification with the mother image." Desmonde spies the paternal influence as he investigates "food rituals" which represent "the breaking through of irrational hostility toward the father" and which are closely associated with money's primitive uses, but that influence, he notes, is properly understood only when regarded in the light of its maternal antecedents. All of this, incidentally, is in accordance with the fact that, in Desmonde's words, "early coins were also amulets, magical devices for retaining the feeling of omnipotence associated with the oral stage."[35] A.C. Haddon, in a non-psychoanalytic survey of primitive money, calls such amulet-coins the "givers of life" in the ancient world.[36] Roheim, who strives to demonstrate that individual economic systems reflect the tensions in the familial organizations of particular cultures, puts the matter this way: "The concept of property, that is, the introjection of part of the external world into the self, comes about through the mediation of a severed part of the body, [and] is tantamount to an erotic tie . . . In those parts of the body that can be severed and are autoerotically cathected, we have the physiological prototype of property." For Roheim the basic psychoanalytic meanings in the whole area of possession and economic organization are to be discovered in the "curious connection between birth and property, between landed property and the mother's body." The "totemistic phase" of primitive society, which stands behind Freud's view of "civilization," has ultimately a *projective* import. It says, "Mother earth belongs to the ancestors, that is, the mother belongs to the father."[37] The fundamental significance is maternal.

Similar items are underscored in Erikson's classic study of the Yuroks, subsequently amplified by Posinsky. The Yuroks are constantly praying for money, not merely because it assists them in creating a ritual atmosphere, but because of what it establishes about them in their own and others' eyes. The possessor of money (in the form of shells) is one who is favored by nature and in particular by the Klamath river, the sacred source of life. Money means communal acceptance, good body contents, and above all, a full mouth.[38] Posinsky declares in this regard, "on a pre-Oedipal level the shell money is certainly equivalent to a positive introject, or 'good body contents;' but it also develops a phallic component which reinforces the previous ones." Thus to be poor originally means "to be hungry or empty," but it also comes to mean "to be without a penis." There is a danger in emptiness *and also* in fullness. The latter derives from the projection of oral aggression onto the parents, and from the "ambivalence involved in fullness" which signifies *both* good and bad body contents. The fear of emptiness makes the Yuroks "greedy and retentive" and the fear of fullness makes them "moderate eaters who must keep the alimentary passage open." The resulting personality is "remarkably akin to a compulsion neurosis." In this way, the "men" of Yurok society are "perpetually involved in Oedipal rivalries," the "never-ending struggle for wealth and prestige."[39]

Such findings call to mind Reich's observation that money and the size of the penis are often equated in the unconscious.[40] Lots of money equals a large penis. But this particular equation has ultimately a transitional significance. When the objects of one's inner world breed insecurity, when one detects the presence of the bad object within, one seeks support, emotive nourishment, or narcissistic supplies in the magical surrogate which actually possesses the power to provide supplies and nourishment in the "real world" and thus comes to be unconsciously associated with the internal system. One is held by money, reassured by money, made secure by money, and this security reaches "up" from the mother to those later "Oedipal rivalries" involving the father and siblings. As Roheim expresses it, "castration anxiety" is ultimately related to the "absence of the mother;" the penis is ultimately a "means of reunion."[41] Thus money, like the penis, is a way back to the object. Even as a source of food it is overdetermined, for as Roheim points out, "the whole process of food distribution--or of wealth or success--is fraught with anxiety."[42] The chief or emperor is sacred because he dispenses food, a function that connects him to God, the provider, on the one hand, and to God's intermediary, the priest, on the other. When medieval Byzantine monarchs, who were *both* sacred and secular rulers, impressed important visitors by showing them "whole roomfuls" of money, they created the impression, writes Michael Hendy, that "between God and the emperor there was no great difference."[43] At the deepest psychoanalytic level, then, money as a means of providing food becomes associated with the entire maternal function, with sustenance, with acceptance, with protection. As for the power of money, it is measured in inner as well as in outer terms that correspond precisely with the context. The powerful, the rich, are *secure*, secure in the tie to the internalized object and in the "reality" which is a projective outgrowth of that tie. Hence, "to distribute things, to feed people, is to be a good mother."[44]

Again and again Roheim stresses the crucial connection between money and the tie to the object, particularly with regard to the central problem of power, or control. "Money gives one control over others, and that is what really tells the story. A lien upon another person means that you can at your will convert him into a giver. The inability to control the mother was the most signal defeat of childhood."[45] To anticipate a thesis, both the power in money generally, and the power-seeking of the capitalist in particular, are related to this preoedipal conflict. The wish is for power that magically fulfills the infantile need to control the maternal figure and her later derivatives. As for the power of the penis and the power of capital, they are also connected thus; both are ways to the object, both are used transitionally to compensate for the "signal defeat of childhood." Stinginess and the compulsive desire for money answer "oral frustrations . . . riches and mother are magically identical . . . to be rich means to be full of good body contents."[46] In this way, the drive for wealth is closely bound up with the unconscious drive for omnipotence. The "cornerstone of the urge to possess," writes Bergler, "is a compensatory mechanism the purpose of which is to heal a wound to the child's self-love, his narcissism,"[47] and the basic wound, the wound which catalyzes the formation of symbols in an effort to internalize the maternal object and thus discover her presence in *other* objects, is separation-in-the-widest-sense, both actual separation and the "fantastic" separation which surrounds the existence of the bad (not-to-be-controlled) object, that is, the frustration and imperfection of the early interaction with the parent. Money "denies dependence," Bergler observes, and "stabilizes feelings of rejection." It is a "blind for existing and repressed infantile conflicts."[48] But as money is also bound up with religious ceremony, and particularly with the practice of *sacrifice*, we had better take a moment to disclose the motivational dynamics of sacrificial behavior and then look at the role of primitive money therein. This will allow us to spy the basic connections between money, religion, and the establishment of ordinary consciousness.

4. The Sacrificial Way to the Object

Hubert and Mauss point out in their definitive study, first, that "sacrifice always implies a consecration; in every sacrifice an object passes from the common into the religious domain; it is consecrated." Second, the consecration "extends beyond the thing consecrated; among other objects, it touches the moral person who bears the *expenses* of the ceremony. The devotee who provides the victim which is the object of the consecration is not, at the completion of the operation, the same as he was at the beginning." He has "acquired a religious character."[49] This acquiring of a religious character, this transformation of the devotee, brings into view the central aim of sacrificial behaviours:

> The thing consecrated serves as an intermediary between the sacrifier,
> or the object which is to receive the practical benefits of the sacrifice,
> and the divinity to whom the sacrifice is usually addressed. Man and
> the god are not in direct contact. In this way, sacrifice is distin-
> guished from most of the facts grouped under the heading of blood
> covenant, in which by the exchange of blood a direct fusion of

human and divine life is brought about. (S, 11)

Thus the chief purpose of sacrifice, which is rooted in an act of "exchange"--the very word Gesell uses to express the chief purpose of money--is *to establish a tie, a connection, a bond,* between the individual who feels the need for such a tie and the divinity to whom he directs his need. In psychoanalytic terms, that divinity is a projective version of the internalized object, a creation which springs from the individual's inner world where an absorption into the bad presence and its derivatives is underway. No longer sure of his inner bearings, experiencing a divisiveness, a self-alienation, a "guilt" that grows as the war between introjections heats up, the devotee seeks to find the good object again and thus to strengthen his internal boundaries by altering the areas in which exchange is occurring. It is not simply the security of the father's good graces that is sought but a deeper security which resides in the deeper layers of personality formation associated with the object of the early time. Thus Hubert and Mauss' description would be both anthropologically and psychoanalytically correct were they to write not of the "fusion" of "human and divine life" that sacrifice strives to bring about but of the *re-fusion* that it seeks.

As for the animal (or "matter") used in the sacrificial action, it is either a "pure" or "sinless" victim, that is, 1) "clean" material offered the divinity in expiation for transgressions committed and designed to facilitate the cleansing of the devotee through his oral or manual touching, or 2) a "tainted" animal, one which, through the ministrations of the priest, bears away the sinfulness of the devotee so as to leave him in a cleansed or pure condition in God's eyes (S, 28-45). This is, of course, a condensation of much material in Hubert and Mauss and leaves out numerous customs and rites. It requires little psychoanalytic knowledge, however, to recognize that the split nature of the victim is a reflection of the split nature of the inner world, forged in the dynamics of internalization. The victim, like the god, is either a version of the good object and its derivatives or the bad object and its derivatives. The tension surrounding the victim reflects the tension which accrues in the ambivalent relationship to the object of the early time whose basic threat is loss, abandonment, rejection, separation. Yet the matter does not end here. So prevalent is this anxiety in infancy that it often gives rise to the fear of engulfment, that is, absorption into the bad object. Thus the sacrificial animal may actually become in the logic of the unconscious a *version of the divinity itself.* The internalized object of infancy is explicitly involved in the projective mechanisms which subsequently handle the conflicts arising from the inner world. In the magic of sacrifice the devotee is offered a safe or "sublimated" avenue to the fulfilment of his incorporative aims. Victim and god are one (Christ as lamb).

When Roy Schafer calls the internalizations of infancy "immortal"[50] he suggests the connection between *that* immortality and the "immortality of the gods." Both are immortal because in ordinary consciousness the transitional aim, the transitional mode of existence, continues throughout life. As Hubert and Mauss express it, "the notion of sacrifice *to* the god developed parallel with that of sacrifice *of* the god" (*S*, 90). Gods do not simply "live" on the substances offered them, they "are born" by them (*S*, 91). The sacrificial substance bears a relation to the life-giving body, and particularly the breast, of life's first object, upon whom the life of the individual depends entirely, just as the inner or even actual life of the sacrificer depends on the refusion with the divinity to whom he addresses himself. When Hubert and Mauss tell us that sacrifice is at the deep psychological level a "guarantee against annihilation" (*S*, 64), they call to mind the annihilation experienced by the infant during periods of separation from, or loss of, the object, and during those periods when he confronts the bad object (often his own "bad" impulses), periods which are also a kind of separation or rejection. The fear of annihilation begins at the beginning and is inextricably bound up with separation from mother at birth and with the inevitable ambivalence of early object relations. Religious and particularly sacrificial activities are employed to cope with that ambivalence, to reestablish equilibrium on the inside and thus preserve order on the outside. One is permitted to indulge his ambivalence in his killing and eating of the victim (scapegoat), yet one is also able to reunite with the good object who, in the magic of the action and through the ministrations of the Priest, will accept one's forbidden desires and judge one "good." Sacrifice enables our repressions, especially repressions of aims associated with the earliest internalizations, to remain flexible and thus preserves social stability by keeping people in contact with their good objects, by making people psychically comfortable in the unity of the dual-unity situation.

Sacrifice, say Hubert and Mauss, "cuts the individual off from the common life, and introduces him step by step into the sacred world of the gods" (*S*, 22). This sacred or magical world into which the individual steps is a "fantastic" version of the "good" world of one's infancy, and its very existence expresses the human need for that good place, for the satisfaction and security which comes at the good breast, and in the body of the good object and her derivatives, the good father, the bosom of Abraham, the protector generally. That which the individual experiences in the "sacred world" is closely related to the "oceanic" experience of union, the "mystical" sense of harmony, merger, well-being which is fundamental to a large area of religious life and feeling.

What all of this makes clear is that religion is a transitional activity designed to accomplish precisely the end accomplished by the transitional object earlier described, the object that "gives" the child to the universe of culture and symbol at the same time that it "takes" the child away from the universe of the mother, the object that magically allows separation and reunion in the same psychological moment. In this way, the sacrificial animal is not simply a special object in the sense that it is a version of the internalized object around which swirls the ambivalence of the early time, the anxiety and hostility tied to loss, rejection, separation, incorporation; it is special too in the sense that it is a version of the transitional object around which swirl those feelings associated with the child's effort to preserve himself, to *retain* himself, during the period in which the crises of separation transpire.

5.   Sacred Lucre

That money plays a central role in sacrificial activity gets not only at the transitional significance of money's complex symbolism but at the extent to which an economic system devoted to the acquisition of money can express transitional aims, can echo the requirements and purposes of the religious system which is ostensibly at odds with the worldly order. That money is inextricably linked in its origin and function to primitive religion and in particular to primitive sacrifice has been indisputably established in the literature and does not require lengthy exposition. Everywhere in primitive culture, writes Einzig, the "sacred" character of money is apparent, as is its role in sacrificial activity.[51] If goods come from god and if money gets goods then money is an integral aspect of god's giving or provision. This insight comes to the members of the group as the emotive aims of sacrifice are accomplished, aims bound up with the "immortal objects" of the inner world. While Weber is correct to suggest that in Protestantism the amassing of wealth, the total concentration upon riches, came to be a way of reaching God and thus, in our terms, a transitional phenomenon with an obsessive or even hysterical cast (the bad object had all but taken over the Puritan), money as a link to god has been there from the beginning; and in the characteristic ambivalence of the human animal toward his projected internalizations, money as the bad object, as filth, has also been there from the beginning, perhaps as a reaction-formation to the deep-seated need for (and fear of) merger.

What constituted the sacrificial animal in Protestantism, the animal offered the deity as the compulsive concentration on work and wealth went forward? What but the body of the Protestant himself, his own body, his own senses? As Weber expresses it,"something more than mere garnishing for purely egocentric motives is involved. In fact, the *summum bonum* of this ethic, the earning of more and more money, combined with the strict avoidance of all spontaneous enjoyment of life, is above all completely devoid of any eudaemonistic, not to say hedonistic, admixture. It is thought of so purely as an end in itself, that from the point of view of the happiness of, or utility to, the single individual, it appears entirely transcendental and absolutely irrational. Man is dominated by the making of money, by acquisition as the ultimate purpose of his life."[52] One's own physical organism, one's own sensuous animal, is rendered up in the magical attempt to reach the transitional god, the sacred lucre.

The psychodynamics of this neurotic behavior emerge more vividly when we recall with Einzig that the word for money in many primitive societies is similar to or even identical with the word *taboo* *(PM*, 72) which means, of course, forbidden or sacred or power-filled or awesome, usually in some religious context. What is desired and pursued is also perceived as dangerous, as reflecting a questionable aim, which focuses from still another angle the ambivalence bound up with the pursuit of wealth,with sacrifice, with religion, and with the internalized objects that are projectively employed as the foundation of these cultural activities. In some areas of the Pacific, *tambu* or money can still be offered the gods in expiation for transgression *(PM*, 72). In ancient Athens money "belonged to" or derived from the mother of the city herself; Athena and her owl are everywhere stamped on the coinage. Rings, too, were frequently used as money in ancient times

(*PM*, 191), and rings are obviously bound up with key transitional phenomena, namely bonding, union, marriage, the sealing of contracts, especially with the paternal or maternal substitute.[53] One is "struck," Einzig remarks, "by the frequent association between primitive money and primitive religion." In many communities the "creation of money is attributed to supernatural powers" (*PM*, 370), for primitive man was guided largely by "religious concerns," and the "evolution of the economic system was itself largely influenced by the religious factor," in particular by the requirements for "sacrifice" (*PM*, 371).

Focusing for us again the transitional significance in Gesell's term "exchange,"as well as the transitional significance of sacrificial conduct generally, Einzig writes in an unforgettable expression that "making sacrifice" to the "deity" is "a form of barter between man and his gods" (*PM*, 371). Not only the sacrificial animal but the very objects employed in the sacrificial action, the knife, the axe, the tripod, the cauldron, the spit, come to be used as money among primitive peoples. Such items created a "unit of account" (*PM*, 73) and might even be *exchanged* for a sacred beast. As for the payment of the priest, it too has clear transitional implications in that the priest is instrumental in establishing the tie between the individual and his god. Today, as the "plate is passed" in church, or metaphorically on television, we recognize how solidly this transitional use of money is established in our own society. One pays, and *then* one gets the good feeling, the sense of connection with and praise from the good object on the inside. As religion evolves, Einzig tells us, "donations to the gods" in the form of "precious metals" (*PM*, 373) become an integral aspect of spiritual life, a traditional part of that "sacrifice" of one's property ("let's all make a sacrifice today") which connects one, or *re*-connects one, with the projective creations of the inner world, with the "divine."

6. Psychodynamic Extrapolations

We are now in a position, I believe, to bring home the full analytic significance of this material, particularly with reference to ordinary consciousness. We must remember that sacrifice is integrally associated with religion's chief aim (refusion), that religion is integrally associated with the sacred, that the sacred is embodied in those symbols (including money) which give a kind of frozen or hieroglyphic expression to mankind's basic conflicts and needs, that the symbolic capacity awakens in people not only through the biological response but in the defensive effort (internalization) to answer the problems of the early time, especially separation, and finally, that our customary method of retaining the tie to the object is to receive and to perceive the universe in a symbolic manner, the manner of ordinary awareness, the manner of language in which, as Aldous Huxley expresses it, "words are taken for things and symbols are used as the measure of reality."[54] In the symbolic mode of ordinary consciousness the very running on of our thoughts, our symbol-thoughts, becomes our way of ensuring what Roheim designated as the central design of culture, namely the establishment of "dual-unity."

Explained here, within the complete historical and anthropological context, of course, is our endless, obsessional pursuit of coin. Because the dual-unity situation is magical, because it has no foundation in actuality, because it is essentially an all-consuming struggle to retain the object, it needs constant support, constant buttressing, constant psychological fuel: one is ultimately in the dependent position on the inside because one is still seeking after the object. When society encourages the strengthening of transitional bonds through the pursuit of wealth by canonizing that pursuit in every imaginable way, the combination of intrapsychic and cultural pressure becomes almost irresistible. Because money functions as an agent of control at the deep psychological level, because money provides the dependent personality with the dream of unlimited power, wealth becomes in the transitional mode a means of accomplishing one's total independence. Were one to possess the object entirely one would not need the object any more. At the same time, because wealth as we know it can only exist in the realm of ordinary awareness, and because ordinary awareness is itself an expression of the tie to and need for the object, the pursuit of coin can only provide an illusory liberation. On the inside the dual-unity situation has not changed. What promises omnipotence ironically makes bondage.

It is interesting in this regard to note the current economic tendency toward the creation of what the experts call "pure money," that is to say, money "in which the medium of exchange function hardly exists."[55] In the words of Walter Neale, "the bulk of modern money--the demand deposits in banks--is not a thing, not a stuff at all, but a set of legally binding statements about rights and obligations. A demand deposit is a promise by the bank to pay the depositor or whomever the depositor orders the bank to pay." Money becomes "disassociated from physical things," and a matter of "promises, promises, nothing but promises."[56] What could be more perfectly designed to engage the world of internalized objects, and in particular, the entire dual-unity situation! One's power, one's control, one's sacred *promise* of reunion, comes not only from the "impure" money in one's pocket but from the "pure" variety that is both present and absent, linked to one and realizable, yet invisible and far away. The shift toward "pure money" may express the modern world's absorption in what Oswald Spengler called in his *Decline of the West* "abstraction;" yet at the same time, it gives unforgettable *psychoanalytic* expression to money's magical character, its capacity to represent the *absent object*, to harbor within its illusory existence those transitional aims which derive from the infant's traumatic *separation* from the parent. What is emerging purely is the pure expression of the human *inner* world.

The connection sought for in sacrifice, the connection with the projective version of the internalized object, the transitional aim of religious behavior accommodated by the transitional employment of money, is ultimately a connection between the individual and the alienated parts of his own body. Religious sacrifice is, in large measure, a way to reach a specific kind of mind-body relaxation in which those parts of the organism that "carry" the internalized object are able to discover a stress-free, harmonious interaction with the rest of the creature. The alienation of "sin" consists largely in the loss of bodily integration, the loss of a happy feeling in the very chemical, physical composition of the self. The sacrificial action leaves the devotee in a relieved, tension-less condition ("now you may relax; everything is going to be all right"), one which may inspire a profound sensation of well-being, of mystical delight, of joyous bodily and spiritual existence. The danger one apprehends in the "sinful" state recalls the danger of the internalized bad object to the infantile body-ego. In a very general sense, unconscious awareness of danger (anxiety) takes the form of stress. The oral significance of sacrifice emerges readily in this context. As one achieves relaxation in the body, as one feels the alienated parts of the organism come together, as one reaches the object one transitionally seeks, as one "regresses" behind the splitting of the early tie toward a harmonious, undifferentiated state of being, one gets the good feed too, the feed associated with the mother's breast, with maternal security and comfort. In Eli Sagan's words, "*all* sacrifice has to do with eating."[57]

As was suggested earlier while discussing the work of Max
Weber, the Protestant sacrifices his body in his all-consuming pursuit of
riches. The traditional use of sacrifice, to render up wealth and to
achieve thereby relaxation in the "new" relationship with the objects of
the inner world, is altered in its unconscious emphases. This is a key
occurrence in the development of western economics. Because the
quest for wealth becomes obsessive, one's body as well as one's money
is used in a transitional way; one's life, as well as one's gold, becomes a
sacrificial entity, which means simply that one holds oneself in tension
and in stress all the time and gets as a reward only the satisfaction that
can arise from the superego which *may* give an affirmative nod to such
a scheme, but well may not, so precarious is the psychological
equilibrium grounded in an ethical system which vehemently pursues a
symbolic version of the mother's body. The peculiar strain of
capitalistic life, a strain that has already contributed to two world wars,
originates in this departure from the normal or "ordinary" use of
religious sacrifice. When one is making a sacrifice of *himself* in his
enormous need for the object, not only is he miserable, he is apt to
make others miserable too.

7. The Metaphors of Marx

I will drive toward the essence of our current religio-economic
order and the patterns of cultures associated with it by examining Karl
Marx' great work, *Das Kapital*, for its metaphorical meanings. I was
always somewhat uncomfortable when listening again and again to the
old cliches--especially popular in North America--that Marx lacked an
understanding of the emotions, that he was rapt in abstractions about
history, that he had little to tell us about the actual, inner workings of
capitalism. This is simply not true. Not only do Marx' writings display
a satirical sharpness and psychological richness that are arresting and
pleasing in themselves, they reveal at the level of figurative language,
the level at which we can feel Marx *intuiting* matters with his whole
responding mind, the *transitional dynamics* of the capitalistic system.
Lenin once remarked (and we may recall here Gesell's point that money
is only a means of exchange), "where the bourgeois economists saw a
relation between things, or the exchange of one commodity for another,

Marx revealed *a relation between people*.[58] In other words, Marx spied the underlying *motivational* significance of the economic setup, and it will be our business, now, to pay attention to his insight.

We must note, first, the language that brings to mind directly the dynamics of sacrificial conduct and money's role therein. The capitalist, in his insatiable greed, is willing to "sacrifice human beings," to "sacrifice" the very "flesh and blood, nerves and brains" of working people in order to maximize his profit, his "surplus-value" which is derived from human labor and which, to this extent, wears a human aspect.[59] Like the Aztecs of old, the owners of industries, the owners of mines and factories, are "prodigal with human lives," casual about "wasting" the men and women to whom they believe they have some sort of natural right. "When profits are at stake," writes Marx, "killing is no murder" (*Kap*, III, 106), just as in the religious sacrifice of human beings killing is also no murder but a "religious" action, that is, an action whose full meaning is concealed beneath the projective defense. In capitalist countries, Marx suggests, human beings are not human beings at all but "horses" whose energy, whose power to make profit becomes the sole concern of the capitalist, who even feeds them certain foods so as to prepare them for their sacred use as begetters of money (*Kap*, I, 627-628). In terms which recall the animal victim of ancient rites, Marx compares the manner in which the "whole beast" is slain in order to provide his owners with a hide to the manner in which the laborer is "converted" or transformed by the capitalist from the human being he is into a kind of "monstrosity" (*Kap*, I, 396), and all for the purpose of providing the capitalist with the gain to whose pursuit he is totally, indeed obsessionally committed. (*Kap*, I, 170).

The figures Marx employs also call to mind the broad mythic framework in which sacrificial conduct transpires, I mean the vegetation myths surrounding the cycle of the seasons, the magical transformations of the year which provide man with his sustenance and which touch directly upon his preoccupation with fertility. To adumbrate a thesis, capitalism in Marx' view perverts the time-honored use of *nature*, the ideal of the production, reproduction, and distribution of nature's goods rooted in the cyclical, vegetational conceptions of the race. "Just as the working day is the natural unit for the function of labor-power," writes Marx, "so the year is the natural unit for the periods of turn-over of rotating capital. The natural basis of this unit is found in the fact that the most important crops of the temperate zone, which is the mother country of capitalist production, are annual products" (*Kap*, II, 176). Thus, the productions of capitalism are linked to the annual or seasonal productions with which men have always associated their religious conception of world process, and more than that, they are linked through the use of a metaphor which calls the mother explicitly to mind, for the heart of the "system" is the crop that arises from the part of the globe which is to be associated with the maternal object herself.

But the workings of capitalism, because they move in a never ending cyclical fashion from year to year, are to be linked not only with the metaphors of production, they are to be linked with the metaphors of reproduction or renewal as well. I do not refer here simply to Marx' use of the expression "industrial cycle" which appears constantly in his work but to other expressions of a related yet qualitatively distinct nature which get at a fundamental figurative aspect of his perception. In words which call up the mythic, vegetative conception of nature in a striking way, Marx writes, "A society can no more cease to produce than it can cease to consume. When viewed, therefore, as a connected whole, as a flowing on with incessant renewal, every social process of production is, at the same time, a process of reproduction" (*Kap*, I, 619-620). Yet the process of reproduction, the renewal process, has embedded in it a further conceptualization of a metaphoric nature which contains a chief preoccupation of Marx throughout the course of *Kapital* and which harbors, perhaps, his richest intuitive insight into the hidden quality of the system. I refer to his tendency to characterize the cycles of capitalism, the processes of "reproduction," in transformational or metamorphic terms that call to mind the basic religious mystery of magical change in which the dead god (cut crop) gives rise to life-producing sustenance, to food. "Production," "consumption," "renewal," "reproduction," "transformation," "metamorphosis," "natural cycle," – these are the key terms of the analysis. Not surprisingly, as we shall see, the final metaphor of the capitalistic system as a whole turns out to be the metaphor of cannibalism in which man's vicious orality, out of control, greedily gulps down the body of the earth itself, the body of the mother-provider.

Embarking upon a discussion of capital's circulation within the system, Marx chooses the following terms to figuratively describe the nature of the item under consideration: "The Metamorphoses of Capital and their Cycles" (*Kap*, II, 31). Everywhere there is talk of transformation: "Productive capital . . . consumes its own component parts for the purpose of transforming them into a mass of products of a higher value" (*Kap*, II, 45). "Labor-power" is "transformed" into "commodity," into the "money-form" (*Kap*, II, 36-37). The "rotation" as a whole comprises the "metamorphoses" of capital, the "transformation" of its "cycle" for the purpose of "making money" (*Kap*, II, 58-59, 60, 67). Capital can "reproduce itself" simply or on an "enlarged scale." "At the end of the period P . . . P, capital has resumed the form of elements of production, which are the requirement for a renewal of its cycle. The rotation of capital, considered as a periodical process, not as an individual event, constitutes its turn-over" (*Kap*, II, 176). But it is perhaps the following example that discloses most vividly this aspect of Marx' figurative language. When "capital" has "finally passed" through "the cycle of its metamorphoses," it "steps forth out of the internal organism of its life" and, like the butterfly emerging from the chrysalis, or the child from the womb, "enters into the external conditions of its existence" (*Kap*, III, 57). Clearly, the cycle of capitalism is modeled upon the cycle of life itself, the fertility cycle traditionally associated with the cycle of the seasons, the "annual cycle," to use Marx' expression again, which is in turn integrally connected with sustenance and which has always been linked at the mythic level to the image of the mother, the mother who is, through a further transformation, *the earth*.

In the transformation of labor into commodity and of commodity into money, money ultimately rooted in the value of labor, Marx uncovered what he took to be the principal "mystery" of the entire "religious" system. Indeed, this transformation, this metamorphosis, to use again Marx' mythic metaphor, is the essence, the ugly, immoral, and destructive essence, of the capitalistic order itself. Insisting that money is a "magical" substance surrounded by illusory thinking, by "necromancy" (*Kap*, I, 87), terms which anticipate Roheim, Marx states that money "contains" nothing other than the "labor," the "power" of men, that has gone into producing the "commodity" which is able to fetch the money in the "market" (*Kap*, I, 93-99). Thus for Marx a "commodity" is, purely and simply, that which holds or "contains" the labor of working people. "Every commodity is a symbol, since, in so far as it is value, it is only the material envelope of the human labor spent upon it" (*Kap*, I, 103). In other words, the commodity, because it harbors "labor," is a symbolic representation of the person, and since it leads to money, *money itself becomes a symbolic representation of the person*, the person who has been *sacrificed* to bring about the magical working of the cycle, the cycle which provides the capitalist with the powerful substance that promises him the fulfillment of his transitional aims and the *cessation of his transitional anxieties*. In Marx' own words, money is entirely and forever in the capitalistic system "the direct incarnation of human labor" (*Kap*, I, 105). The capitalist invests in the "very flesh and blood of the laborers" (*Kap*, III, 158). Through the unconscious, defensive *disguise* of the cyclical order, then, the capitalist devours the bodies of his workers in an unholy version of religious sacrifice. His money is his *feed*, and as Marx sees it at the level of symbolic representation, the feed is upon an object that contains the body of the worker himself in a hidden or metamorphosed form acceptable to the conscience of the owner.

At the level of *conscious* process, however, the capitalist regards "surplus-value" as the "offspring" of his monetary resources (*Kap*, III, 49), and the "breeding of money" becomes his obsessive concern (*Kap*, III, 462). Indeed, after a certain period of time has elapsed, the investor considers his "money" to be "pregnant" (*Kap*, III, 462). Interest and profit "accumulate," and finally "fulfill" his most "fervent wish" (*Kap*, III, 462). The "social powers of production," accordingly, "sprout from the womb of capital itself" (*Kap*, III, 963) and *not* from the bodies of men and women. It is an "old story," declares Marx, "capital begets capital" as "Abraham begat Isaac," and "Isaac begat Jacob," and "so on" (*Kap*, I, 637). The sacred nature of capitalist ideology begins to reveal its origin. Just as the symbols of the *religious* system deal with or cope with the basic transitional anxieties of men, so do the symbols of the economic system, the "other side" of religion, its "opposite," its unconscious *double*, deal with or cope with those anxieties. In *both realms* the symbol leads to the projective version of the internalized parent which is in the last analysis the *sacred*. In religion money is used in sacrifice to gain control over or reunion with the "lost" object. In *economics*, which transpire in "society," in the "real" world, man is used sacrificially to obtain the money, to obtain the "gold," which unconsciously represents the security, the power, the potency, required by the individual in the "dual-unity situation," in the transitional mode of existence, in the "reality" of separation from the object. Money means control over the extension of the parent, for that is what "society" is. As we have seen, the tie to the social order, to "civilization," is an outgrowth of the tie to the internalized object. The "religious world," said Marx in what is perhaps his most famous utterance, "is but a reflex of the real world." The full, *unconscious* meaning of this statement derives from Marx' own *metaphoric* examination of capital.

8. The Interest in Interest

The association of *interest* and *time* is of course fundamental to the system, and Marx acknowledges it at the inception of his discussion. But the time bound up with interest is for Marx dependent upon the time bound up with the rate of capital turnover as a whole, and in this respect his analysis leaves far behind those who suggest that time begets interest in a simple, straightforward way. He writes, "With his customary insight into the internal connection of things, the romantic Adam Muler says: 'In determining the prices of things, time is not considered; while in the determination of interest it is principally time which is taken into account.' He does not see that the time of production and the time of circulation enter into the determination of the price of commodities, and that this is precisely what determines the rate of profit for a given time of turn-over of capital, while the determination of profit for a certain time in its turn determines that of interest" (*Kap*, III, 420). Interest, therefore, is a "part of profit," of "surplus-value," and is always to be "measured in money" (*Kap*, III, 421) or in the labor of men of which money is a "crystallized form." Interest goes "down" in prosperous times as "extra profit" and up in times of crisis during the course of which it may reach "a point of extreme usury" (*Kap*, III, 424). These are, in the last analysis, but aspects of the industrial cycle: "condition of rest, increasing activity, prosperity, over productivity, crises, stagnation, condition of rest, etc." (*Kap*, III, 424). How does this material shed light upon the *transitional* nature of the search for gain?

Interest is not simply an aspect of *profit*, it is that aspect of profit which is *entirely associated* with the passage of *time* in the industrial cycle. As we have seen, time is from a psychoanalytic angle inextricably bound up with the infant's relation to the maternal object. Indeed, the coming and the going of the mother is the principal event in the rudimentary growth of the time sense. Security becomes the mother's presence measured in terms of inchoate duration, and "good eternity" is in large measure the blissful sense of timeless well-being experienced in the longed-for union with the breast. It is in the intervals of the mother's absence that imaging achieves intensity as an aspect of the internalizing, symbol-making capacity which is, in turn, the organism's way of *holding* the mother during those periods when she is not there. Prolonged absence on the mother's part becomes an experience of catastrophic dimension for the infant and is closely connected to the individual's apprehension of "bad" time, or "bad eternity," a feature of Hell.

The transitional meaning of interest as profit emerges from this perspective. Because interest provides money, because it leads to money after a period of waiting, and because money is a symbol rooted in the drive to control and reunite with the internalized object, interest becomes a kind of psychological scheme to fill time with the magical presence of the maternal figure. One is making money as time passes and to this extent the emptiness of time is denied, the absence of the object is denied; indeed, the emptiness of time and the object's absence are only *illusions*. Time is not simply passing, it is breeding money, money which makes one secure in its passing. Thus the interest in interest attests to the individual's desire to be imaging unconsciously the object of one's security *all the time*, just as the child has the mother *all the time* at the level of his primary, internalized *holding*. The feed of cash proceeds uninterruptedly at the level of transitional need. One "goes through life" with his lips at the breast. These lines of Dylan Thomas get at the matter effectively:

> The lips of time leech to the fountainhead,
> Love drips and gathers, but the fallen blood
> Shall calm her sores. 60

And when the sum of interest actually appears, when the "payoff" actually arrives, it constitutes not only the climax to a period of passive ingestion, passive sucking, it constitutes as well the proof that the "stuff" was there. One's good anticipation leads to one's gratification "in reality." Time, intimately associated with the threat of loss, has been mastered. At the level of unconscious processes, the accumulation of interest is a secular version of eternal life.

9. The Vicious Circle and the Bad Parent

The psychological feed of interest calls to mind once more the agrarian features of Marx' approach, his association of capitalism with the "cycle of production" in its mythic or archetypal form. I want at this point to focus on what might be termed the final metaphors of Marx' analysis and, in this way, bring my examination of *Das Kapital* to a close.

Capitalism for Marx is not simply a version of the "annual cycle," it is the vicious version, the evil version, undermining and destroying the ancient wisdom expressed through the myth in its ideal, pristine expression. The "annual" productions of "nature" which beget the "general stock" of society are *unnaturally* handled; they are "retained" for the private, egoistical use of the capitalist, and thus the yearly "cycle" becomes a destructive instrument, one that breeds injustice and suffering instead of abundance and well-being (*Kap*, I, 533). Marx stated this even more dramatically in the notebooks from which he drew the material for *Das Kapital*: "The circle Money-Commodity-Money, which we drew from the analysis of circulation, would then appear to be merely an arbitrary and senseless abstraction, roughly as if one wanted to describe the life cycle as Death-Life-Death."[61] Referring caustically to the orthodox "Political Economy" of his day, Marx declares that the "vicious circle" of "capitalist production" may be traced *not* to a "system" of "primitive accumulation" but to the *feudal system* in which the control and exploitation of man and nature was more visible, more open, less "mystified" than in the present mode (*Kap*, I, 784-786). As for that system's "lord," he becomes in the course of industrial development the "new potentate" of the capitalistic order (*Kap*, I, 786).

The "vicious circle" which Marx describes appears to those who cannot see into the realities of production as a "natural" system using "natural resources." He writes, "Because this power costs capital nothing, and because, on the other hand, the labourer himself does not develop it before his labour belongs to capital, it appears as a power with which capital is endowed by Nature--a productive power that is immanent in capital" (*Kap*, I, 365). But for all its "naturalness" capitalism ultimately "perverts" nature and the order of life, the benign, provisional earthly cycle expressed in the myths which celebrate the world's miraculous, divine ability to provide men seasonally with nourishment, to act as *good* feeder, *good parent*, by *transforming* the seed into the crop or by offering substances that might *be* transformed into food through specific ministrations, such as heat. Capitalism is thus not only a *bad* feeder, a *bad* distributor at the individual level, it is threat to the survival of mankind as a *family*, as a society; it is a threat to the globe: "Capitalism loses on one side for society what it gains on the other for the individual capitalist" (*Kap*, III, 104). The "transformation" of "surplus-value" into"profit" is a "perversion of subject and object taking place in the process of production" (*Kap*, III, 58). The "real barrier of capitalist production is capital itself. It is the fact that capital and its self-expansion appear as the starting and closing points, as the motive or aim of production; that production is merely production for capital, and not vice versa, the means of production mere means for a never expanding system of life process for the benefit of the society of producers" (*Kap*, III, 293). In times of crisis, and here again the agrarian metaphor peeks through, "old capital" is compelled to "lie fallow;" production "stagnates;" the capitalists begin to war among themselves: "How much the individual capitalist must bear of the loss . . . is decided by power and craftiness, and competition then transforms itself into a fight of hostile brothers" (*Kap*, III, 296-297).

The figure of "hostile brothers" is integrally bound up with Marx' explicit presentation of the capitalist himself as the *bad parent*, as one who has failed to achieve psychological maturity, as one who remains at the level of sibling-rivalry as opposed to the level of parental responsibility, as one who provokes transitional anxiety in the working classes the members of which *grip the economic system for reasons similar to those for which they grip ordinary awareness*, and who view the owner with a deep-seated *ambivalence* similar to that with which the owner views *them*. The medieval "lord" is also the *bad object*, a reflection of Plutus, god of the underworld (*Kap*, I, 148-149). "Certain individuals," writes Marx, claim to have an "exclusive right" to "certain pieces of the globe" (*Kap*, III, 743), and in the process of turning these "pieces" to their own advantage they negate an ancient purpose. No one, he declares, "owns" the earth. We all simply "use" it; and our business is to use it justly so that we may distribute its products to all who presently require them, thus preserving the planet for succeeding generations. To do this is, in Marx's words, to behave ourselves as "the good father of a family behaves himself" (*Kap*, III, 902).

Marx' depiction of the capitalist as *bad parent* is tightly related to his picture of the earth under the spell of the capitalist order, a picture in which the planet is wasted and destroyed by the irresponsibilities of the obsessive, egocentric owners, in which the "annual cycle" of abundance grinds to a terrible halt. The world becomes a permanent wasteland; the ancient wisdom which men have heeded since "time immemorial" is lost (*Kap*, III, 961). The "lord" of the "unnatural" system enters the "bowels of the earth" and takes from them the source of mankind's future wealth; he drains the very "body" (*Kap*, III, 898) of the globe, "consumes" the very "fruits of the earth," and in this way leaves it "barren," a place of "soil" that is finally "exhausted" (*Kap*, III, 946). What is particularly striking about this is Marx' employment of *oral* metaphors which get further at the *transitional* significance of the "vicious circle." It is at the oral level that Marx spies the danger, for it is the capitalist's "all-engrossing appetite" (*Kap*, III, 466) that "consumes" the earth's products, that empties the mother's "body." Left unchecked, writes Marx, the capitalist would simply "eat up the world" (*Kap*, III, 463), devour it, cannibalize it; his conduct marks him as a kind of "wolf" or "shark" (*Kap*, III, 520-521) with an endless hunger for victims. Thus Marx is ultimately disgusted and outraged by capitalism's *greedy mouth*, its narcissistic orality which has no respect for the careful approach of the old tradition.

Just as splitting, internalization, ambivalence, and refusion constitute keys to the religious activities of people in which money and sacrifice play a crucial role, so do they constitute keys to the economic activities of people in which money and sacrifice also figure centrally. And if the bonds of "civilization" and "religion" are rooted in the tie to the parent, then the bond between the capitalist and his economic order, his secular "religion," his "theology" of the marketplace, is also rooted in that tie. Nor can the psychological forces which bind the workers to the "system" be ignored here, for the worker too is prone to regard the economic setup as an aspect of the "civilization" to which he is linked at the emotive level, the level of *transference* relations, the level at which he is ultimately linked to his ordinary manner of perception itself. *All* of these "phenomena," economic, religious, and perceptual, are aspects of a single issue: man's tendency to internalize his environment, to cope with his intense transitional anxiety by exploiting his biological proclivity to create symbols, to "get on top" of his world by transforming it into concepts which are charged with projective, defensive energy. The separation crises of infancy and childhood unite with the symbol-making brain to produce the transitional mode of "civilization," the mode which defines the present perceptual stage of the species.

10. More Opiates, More Anxieties:
The Economic System Today

The capitalist of the nineteenth century subscribed to the notion that his economic activity was subject to the authority of the market. Today, although a few diehards still cling to this view, the vast majority have come to recognize that we live, and *must* live, in a planned economy. Manufacturing, mining, electric power, communications, transportation, a good portion of the retail trade, and even the entertainment industry, are controlled by several hundred large firms that work closely with government to bring about what is called "the general prosperity." It is the *planning* of these "giants" that ensures their unhindered expansion and success. The large corporation strives to control the supply of raw materials, for example, by extending its activities into areas out of which it formerly kept. Instead of haggling with the supplier, it becomes the supplier; instead of waiting upon workers of other firms to iron out their problems with their bosses, it buys the firms; instead of struggling to obtain capital, it creates its own capital and thus excludes outsiders; instead of waiting to see whether or not the public will purchase its products, it advertises on a massive scale so that they *will* purchase them; instead of praying that the government will not interfere with its activities, it aligns itself with government through joint investment and makes the well-being of the state dependent on its own well-being. In addition to all this, it influences legislation to make the tax burden fall on those from whom it actually derives its profit. Everything is arranged. Nothing is left to chance, as far as this is humanly possible. In the words of John Galbraith, "from the time and capital that must be committed, the inflexibility of this commitment, the needs of the large organization and the problems of market performance under conditions of advanced technology, comes the necessity for planning. Tasks must be performed so that they are right not for the present but for that time in the future when, companion and related work having also been done, the whole job is completed."[62] Nearly every facet of our current economic system can be traced to this method of "doing business."

I have three points here: first, current economic procedures are designed to master aspects of economic *anxiety* that are characteristic of capitalist enterprise; second, those who attend the corporate power structure are committed to controlling and manipulating "the public" (including the workers) in the course of their efforts to flourish; and third, the end of all this planning, all this "sophisticated" economic activity, is exactly what it was during earlier periods, namely the acquisition of *money*. As for the *meaning* of money today, it represents precisely what it represented in Marx' day, and in days long before that, namely *power*, power over people and events, power that ultimately springs from the labor of human beings, the individuals who make the system "go."

The "modern" capitalist has had time to learn what is likely to impede the satisfaction of his transitional needs, and he has striven to remove such impediments, much as the child learns to master the "reality" that interferes with the satisfaction of his own aims. Grown up at the "top," the capitalist has remained exactly the same at the "bottom." He is devoted to the endless acquisition of wealth and to the control that such wealth brings. Taught unforgettably by the Great Depression, or as it is called, the Great *Panic*, that his "system" *could* break down, that the transitional feed of riches *could* be interrupted, he strove to devise methods for completing his mastery and assuring thereby his longed-for security. The capitalist's "opium," his "hit," is the same today as it was before; today, however, he makes sure of his supply. Indeed, profits themselves are limited *by* the industrial system so as to provide a steady flow and a steady expansion, so as to *protect* the owner against the *loss* that might occur in a free and open market. Even the body of labor, formerly the target of scornful confrontation, is treated in a manner that lessens the possibility of radical, long-term disruption. Although he knows the state will give him preferential treatment in its dependence on a capitalist economy, the owner works to see "force," and its "formal constitution as political power," applied shrewdly, even sensitively, so that "labor-power may be held in place,"[63] available to the servicing of his needs. Thus the *profit-making* of the present setup recalls the *interest-making* of Marx' day: to master *time*, to *control the future*, to ensure the steady, uninterrupted flow of gain, to fill the anxious emptiness with the mother's presence--these appear to be the central goals of the system.

That the capitalist's new methods have actually diminished his anxiety is highly improbable; in all likelihood they have only increased it. The need to control breeds uncertainty, breeds doubt, breeds an ever-greater desire for control, for *more control*. No matter how much one tries, one cannot be *sure*. And bigger investments mean potentially bigger catastrophes. Planning is not only essential, it is difficult as well, for a great many things can go wrong. *Always* the underlying possibility of disaster is there. Psychoanalysis has taught us that one can "get hooked" on being anxious, on being in the "state" one has grown up with and gotten used to. It calls this condition the "repetition compulsion." Paradoxically, the capitalist's security is *assured* by his planning and *removed* by his planning. As Michael Harrington expresses it, "capitalist life is particularly schizophrenic" in that the "system" is "increasingly scientific as to details" but "irrational as a totality."[64] The attempt to do the impossible, *to control the entire market*, speaks not only for the disturbance in the behavior but for the *transitional* purpose in the behavior as well. One *will* be secure in an uncertain world. One *will* have the riches that mean control and refusion. Time *will* succumb to the manipulations of "reason." Here is the old *religio-economic* impulse in all its unconscious urgency. However, transitional aims impel not only the owners and executives at the top of the technostructure, they impel the managers and workers at the middle and lower levels as well. Large, complex entities, corporations urge employees to *identify* with company goals, to emotionally join the organizational *family* with which they are in daily association. The individual comes to think of himself as a General Motors man, or a Prudential man, or a Sears man. In addition, because the corporation has come to recognize that the "loyalty" of the employee *increases* through "decent treatment," through a "living wage" and "security benefits," and that such "loyalty" is *good for profits*, it has acted accordingly, *which has had the effect of deepening one's identification with the company*. People become *psychically* tied to their "positions." They surrender to the organization because they believe it can do more for them than they can do for themselves. Identification permits the magical conviction that *they too* are reaching the transitional goals after which the corporation chases; they too are part of the large, powerful "structure" that gets the huge wealth and that, in association with other large "structures," other large surrogates, controls "reality," or "the world." Money received in wages derives from *this source* and thus provides, in the fantastic arrangement characteristic of our era, not only an avenue back to the maternal figure but a "part" of that figure herself. Indeed, employees are nudged in this psychological direction by management's proferring token shares in the company, actual "pieces" of the corporate "body." Each worker is transformed into a little capitalist, and the system as a whole is characterized less by war between rival segments of society than by identification within one large "capitalist" class.

For all this, of course, the "order" is essentially the same as it was during earlier decades. It has merely softened relations to get cooperation. The worker is still exploited, as he was in the nineteenth century. His exploitation is simply concealed by propaganda, by shibboleths, by a car in the garage, a chicken in the pot, a union contract, two weeks of leisure, and perhaps a few shares of stock (this in "good" countries and "good" times; in "bad" countries and/or "bad" times things are very different). *His capacity to identify with symbols of power is exploited along with his labor.* Before he was simply "skinned." Now he is psychologically seduced *and* skinned. I believe he had more dignity before.

Moreover, for all the softening of industrial relations, for all the "benefits" accorded "working people," the rape of the earth, the despoliation and debasement of the planet, the egocentric pursuit of wealth and the inequitable distribution of resources, in a word, the perversion of the ancient wisdom embodied in the agrarian myths, are every bit as visible in our own time as they were in the time of *Das Kapital*, and perhaps even *more* visible if one has the ability to see through the fulsome, propagandistic screens of the large corporations ("Finding new energy for *you!*" "We *care* for our customers!"). As in the past, human beings are infantalized on an enormous scale, urged to exist in a transitional attitude toward creation, still seeking the parental figure, still clinging to ordinary reality, still tied to the forces of the inner world, still wasting their power on the surrogate objects of the marketplace. Identification with the corporate structure, or with the state of which it forms an integral part, does not change the result, for identification is by definition a transitional behavior. One cannot have *himself* when he belongs to another *power*, either through coercion, as in Marx' day, or through identification as in our own. Writes Galbraith: "What is the question automatically asked when two corporate employees meet on a plane? 'Who are you with?' Until this is known the individual is a cipher. He cannot be placed in the scheme of things." Of executives in particular, Galbraith notes that they often demand, "How can you overwork if your work is your life?"65 When an individual maintains that his work is his *life*, one can safely replace "life" with another word, for there is only one "object" in one's "life" that is *that* important, and the needs associated with her are frequently transferred to one's precious employment. Additionally, the word "life" as it is used in the foregoing passage focuses the element of *sacrifice*, with its multiple religious and transitional meanings, in the current economic order.absorbed in his responsibilities, the corporate executive is eager to devote his energy, his power, his body, his very "life" to the imposing "structure" of which he forms a "part."

11. Lurking Ambivalence

I would not want in all of this to suggest that the employee's identification with the company is an unambivalent one. Relationships rooted powerfully in internalized objects will always evince ambivalence, as well as corresponding projections in "reality." Among those who have little, and *can have* but little, namely the workers, such ambivalence is often apparent, overt, outspoken. Not only is dispossession a barrier to identification but exposure to anti-establishmentarian ideas may well foster opposition to the system and gravitation toward a "radical" party--frequently fated to become a *transitional* entity itself, as has The Party in the Soviet Union. But the ambivalence is commonly discovered in higher-ups as well.

The procedures and techniques associated with mass production, writes Pederson-Krag in a pioneering discussion, foster in the employee a kind of "existential fatigue" by according him a "status" that corresponds in the unconscious to the "conditions of infancy."66 Although the individual is integrated into the organizational structure, he is also obliged to undergo the reactivation of unpleasurable affect, a considerable amount of it in fact. The relationship between people "is based on fear of aggression from strangers," that is, competing companies, which makes each person "submit to the authority of his superior." Superintendents urge subordinates to work more efficiently so as to surpass the output of other firms, and "this is the equivalent of stimulating the workers' rivalry with unknown competitors to overcome their resentment of authority and aversion to effort." Pederson-Krag goes on, "superintendents report to the manager of a department which produces either one complicated product or several of the same nature. The manager is subordinate to a vice-president who surveys not only manufacturing but allied problems such as cost, design, and demand. The president gives an account of the whole procedure to the chairman of his board of directors." The organization resembles "the feudal system," with the "squire commanding the peasants, the baron the squires" until the "final authority, the king," is reached. And then, in a key observation, "the corporation is like *a vast pregenital mother* who gives her brood security and nourishment, but who loves the eldest and strongest (the top executives) best, since she gives them the most. The weaker and inexperienced newcomers get promotion and wage increases, favors from the mother, only if they are deserving and their superiors approve." As for the junior executives, although they express their rivalry toward colleagues, they prefer a "protecting, maternal organization to independence." When the "pregenital mother plays favorites" and becomes "too closely identified with the strong men" at the top, a "new mother, the union, takes her place" and "forces her to feed the hungry young." Clearly then, while the corporation is gripped in a transitional way, there is plenty of ambivalence and fear in the gripping. Adhered to and "loved" for its "bodily contents," it is vilified and hated for its debasing, authoritarian method of organizing human relations.

A similar ambivalence is directed toward the state as *it* strives to cope with the tensions of the religio-economic system, the tensions inherent in the distribution of money and power. As we noted in an earlier paragraph, the state is predisposed to accord preferential treatment to the capitalist upon whom its own prosperity ultimately depends. At the same time, it is obliged to *legitimate* its actions to the populace from whom it derives its political existence in the first place. Hence the state, or as we may think of it in the western world, the welfare state, is perforce involved in specific and persistent "contradictions" which call to mind the contradictions just ascribed to the pregenital corporate mother. The writings of Claus Offe are especially effective on this score.

"What the state protects and sanctions," Offe observes, "is a set of institutions and social relationships necessary for the domination of the capitalist class." Yet it also seeks to "implement and guarantee the collective interests of all members of a class society dominated by capital." The "structural contradictions" involved in this are plain: to the extent that state policies serve the interests of the populace they "burden the owners of capital;" to the extent that they give preferential treatment to the owners they negate the demands of the populace. Thus the state "does not so much, as liberal reformers believe, become a force of social change and social progress, but rather it increasingly becomes the arena of struggle. It provides the rudimentary model of organization of social life that is liberated from the commodity form without being able to live up to the promise implicit in that model." Indeed, notes Offe, "state agencies project an image of themselves that suggests that use values like education, knowledge, health, welfare and other ingredients of a 'decent' life actually are the final purpose of its measures and policies. The experience that this image is misleading, and that the state produces all these services not in order to satisfy the corresponding needs, but only to the extent that it is required to keep in motion the universe of commodities with its implicit exploitative relationships of production--this experience must cause specific conflicts and attitudes of frustration over 'false promises.' "[67] In this way, the state takes up its symbolic, psychoanalytic place along side Marx' capitalist "bad parent" and Pederson-Krag's "corporate mother" to elicit the unconscious conflicts of millions of individuals who are in the transitional mode of awareness and thus prone to transfer their transitional longings to those entities in the external world that reactivate the primary *struggle* of the original object relation.

When the state favors the owners it becomes the bad, rejective object of the workers and populace, the object that *promises* "good body contents" but fails to deliver them (anything less than total commitment can mean rejection and abandonment in the infantile unconscious). When the state favors the workers and populace it becomes the bad, rejective object of the owners, the object that impedes their chase after *riches*, the substitutive "stuff" which comprises their precious narcissistic supply and for which they *sacrifice* their lives. Those who rely on "welfare," who see the world ideally as a place that provides security and peace, who want *that* version of the object, resent the policies that favor those who view the world more aggressively, those who would *gain* the object through compensatory phallic striving, those who would *take others over, incorporate other corporations, other corporate bodies*, and who view the populace with their "welfare mentality" as feckless children (or "sibling rivals") sucking at the tit of the nation's resources. Just as the actual maternal object was not *fair*, just as *she promised* symbiosis and then enforced *separation*, just as *she* became involved in "structural contradictions," or "contradictions" that emerged during the course of one's *structural, psychological development*, so the state is not *fair*, so the state makes *promises* that it *can not* keep, so the state is involved in fundamental contradictions that affect its distribution of sacred lucre and the economic power to *get* it. While it may be correct to say that both the corporation and the state contribute to the current form of "domination," we must remember that the initial and primal domination of human experience is the domination of the individual by the objects within, the "immortal objects" whose persistent, implacable influence stands squarely behind those forms of domination that eventually characterize the social world in which the individual comes to have his "mature" existence. Everyone--owners, bureaucrats, workers--is ultimately trapped in the transitional mode of awareness, the *engenderer* of the projective malaise that comprises the current religio-economic system with its domestic and international tensions. A "perfected state" in which "reasonable people live together"[68] may come if it comes at all *after* the transitional mode has been fully grasped and modified.

12. Goods and More Goods

Our analysis would be conspicuously incomplete were it to overlook *consumerism*, that aspect of the present order which directly engages the citizenry as a whole. What emerges here is plain enough: everything in the system, and that includes the state, is geared toward manipulating the "consumer" into a steady, uninterrupted urge to *buy products*, to *possess things*. Indeed, it is precisely this manipulation that stands at the center of the entire setup. To accomplish such an end, to "bring it off," the controllers of the marketplace must create the illusion that nothing is going on out there except the exercise of choice, that the individuals in the society, the *targets*, are entirely free to make their own decisions. "It is possible," writes Galbraith, "that people need to believe that they are unmanaged if they are to be managed effectively."[69] When we examine this "management" even briefly we realize that it takes the form of an unflagging propaganda on behalf of goods. Again in the words of Galbraith, "from early morning until late at night, people are informed of the services rendered by goods--of their profound indispensibility. Every feature and facet of every product having been studied for selling points, these are then described with talent, gravity, and an aspect of profound concern as the source of health, happiness, social achievement, or improved community standing. Even minor qualities of unimportant commodities are enlarged upon with a solemnity which would not be unbecoming in an announcement of the combined return of Christ and all the apostles. More important services, such as the advantages of whiter laundry, are treated with proportionately greater gravity. The consequence is that while goods become ever more abundant they do not seem to be any less important. On the contrary, it requires an act of will to imagine that anything else is so important."[70] The point is, goods are what the industrial system supplies. Advertising, by making goods important, makes the industrial system important and thus sustains the social significance, the prestige, of the corporate structure. Because the well-being or "health" of the "economy" is totally dependent upon the public's continuous *expenditure* of money it is vital not merely to get people to spend, it is dangerous to allow them to *save*. It is by *consuming products* that individuals serve the industrial order. The very system of taxation itself, and even the rate of inflation, are managed to ensure a steady rate of profit to the companies, and in this, of course, the *state* lends its support. In a very real sense, it *plans* the savings of its "citizens."

Most goods, needless to say, are not required in any genuine material sense; they have primarily a psychic appeal. They provide a sense of personal accomplishment, or equality with the neighbors; they "take one's mind off things," or enhance confidence in the sexual sphere. "The industrial system serves wants which are psychological in origin and hence admirably subject to management. Although a hungry man cannot be persuaded as between bread and a circus, a well-nourished man can . . . The further a man is removed from physical needs the more he is open to persuasion--or management--as to what he buys. This is, perhaps, the most important consequence for the economics of increasing affluence."[71] Surely one cannot miss the *transitional* significance in all of this. To go to the heart of the matter, capitalism in its present form *exploits the psychological equivalence of money and goods* in such a way as to lay the accent on goods, goods which *represent money*, which are money at the level of unconscious mentation. As Roheim observed, it is not merely "coin" as such that comes to signify the body of the object, either as a direct substitute (in primitive culture) or as a symbol of control (in the capitalist era). Wealth *in any form* can serve the magical purpose of dual-unity by becoming a surrogate for the maternal figure. It is precisely in this sense that the Marxian transformation of commodity into riches not only remains with us but expands to include the manner in which the citizenry as a whole is "skinned." The *transitional circle* of the industrial state *closes* through the identification of the employee *and* the consumer with symbols the maternal or "religious" signification of which is apparent--the corporate body and *what comes from it*, its *product*, its "content." An entire population, directly under the influence of state and private management, struggles to fulfill its transitional needs and to allay its transitional anxieties through, on the one hand, identification with the corporate structure and, on the other, the expenditure of a substance which begets in return but a version of itself.

Remarkably, then, it is not only the worker who is transformed into a little capitalist; *everyone* in this "one-dimensional" system undergoes the transformation. The emotional malaise which Marx discovered in the character of the "primitive" capitalist (oral devourer, shark) spreads through the whole population. Exploited for profit and, *at the same time*, given access to "goods," each member of the order is strenuously encouraged to pursue the transitional dream. Not only can *everyone* have a chicken in the pot, *everyone* can possess the traditional symbols of the owner (symbols that signify power and security) in their fake, middle-class form: a big, cheap version of a luxury carriage (the "motor car"), an imitation-crystal chandelier, a credit-card that speaks for hidden resources, for "backing," a neighborhood home with a "plantation" facade, many pairs of shoes, jewelry. The "passionate chase after riches" which formerly characterized the capitalist becomes the passionate chase after *goods* which presently characterizes the consumer. Existence is *sacrificed* to the begetting of *possessions* which, in contrast to religion, become the new "opium" of the industrial community.

It all seems perfectly natural, of course; not simply because the transitional longings are real (and endless), but because *both* sides of the power structure receive a transitional reward, a transitional "hit. The owner gets his profit, the consumer gets his stuff. But the system is natural only in the way in which labor power appeared natural in Marx' own day. To grasp the system in its underlying meaning is to grasp its infantilism, its wastefulness, its danger to the development of the species, its irrational, "religious" character. When Galbraith tells us that laundry soap is advertised with a seriousness that would be appropriate to the return of Christ and the apostles there is more than a rhetorical truth in the comparison. "If we continue to believe," he writes, "that the goals of the industrial system--the expansion of output, the companion increase in consumption, technological advance, the public images that sustain it--are coordinate with life, then all of our lives will be in the service of these goals."[72] One could not wish for a sentence that more vividly points up the compensatory, sacrificial, sacred nature of the order. Everywhere beneath the surface of the entire "organization" the quest for transitional reward is visible.

The ubiquitous "public images" which support the industrial system provide still another insight into the transitional nature of this questing. Goods are not offered to the populace simply as personalized indications of power and security, as psychological avenues to transitional fulfillment at the level of individual desire; goods are offered in such a way as to become loved and worshipped as symbols of the *national purpose*. In the prevailing ideology of the industrial state, what the corporation produces, what the consumer purchases, and what the nation is accomplishing are connected inextricably at the emotional level. Our current social organization, our current "democracy," Eli Sagan reminds us, "is the least dependent upon fundamental kinship ties of any political system ever invented, and as a result it generates an unusual share of anxiety, paranoia, and the need to express aggression outward, toward the world." Sagan also observes, "slowly and painfully, society has been attempting over thousands of years to construct new forms of attachment and reassurance that would compensate us for our kinship paradise lost."[73] The link between the modern economic setup and what this paragraph describes as the "national purpose" is solidified by these statements. Our passionate chase after *goods* ("good objects") is, first, our attempt to discover "new forms of attachment" in our alienated, kin-less culture, our paradise *lost*. We shop, we buy, we *consume*, we feed ourselves "products," in a pathetic, obsessive struggle to deny the absence of those flesh-and-blood contacts that formerly tied people together and provided them with precious compensation for the *loss* of the object which characterized the separation phase of infancy. Second, we make our obsessive economic activity, our endless oral frenzy, a part of the "national purpose," or indeed the national purpose *itself* ("the richest country in the world!"), in an effort to convince ourselves that we do in fact live in a genuine society, in a truly cohesive group, in a shared community of emotion and purpose. We know deep down, however, that loneliness and isolation are the rule.

Richard Koenigsberg writes in his book, *The Psychoanalysis of Racism, Revolution, and Nationalism*, "where once the individual's connection to the community had been defined in terms of relationships with persons *present* in the immediate physical environment, now this connection is defined in terms of relationships with persons *not present* in the immediate physical environment." Koenigsberg goes on, "there are a number of important changes which are associated with this shift in the nature of community. One of the most important of these . . . is that a national community may be more easily 'turned off' than a physically present community. If one does not wish to 'interact' with one's 'friends' from the mass-media, one may turn off the television, stop reading newspapers, etc."[74] What this brings home vividly is the following: It is not merely *goods* that serve a transitional purpose in our current, "loose," democratic society; the media in the widest sense, television, newspapers, magazines, films, *all* the "non-present" forms of attachment, serve such a purpose as they foster the so-called global village. We do not turn to these entities and then away from them again in pure, conscious *choice*. We turn to and away in *compulsion*, in *ambivalence*, in *confusion*, and even in *sorrow*. We turn to and away because these "non-present" forms mirror or reflect the nature of our ordinary awareness in a deep psychological way. The psyche may grow toward individuation, and this may destroy the old kinship bonds and the direct, supportive style of social interaction. But the psyche does not relinquish its transitional intention, its life and death struggle to hold on to the object and its concomitant tendency to *project* that struggle into its environmental creations. We are dealing here with a *whole perceptual orientation* that is ultimately *symptomatic* in nature. We are dealing with the human organism as a receiver and perceiver of the universe. *This* is the issue.

Notes and References

Part Two

1. Freud, Sigmund. *The Future of an Illusion*, trans. W. D. Robson-Scott. New York: Anchor Books, 1953, p. 4.
2. *Ibid.*, p. 41.
3. Piaget, Jean. *Six Psychological Studies*, trans. Anita Tenzer. New York: Vintage Books, 1967, p. 9.
4. Freud, Sigmund. *The Future of an Illusion*, ed. cit., p. 110.
5. Brown, Norman O. *Life Against Death*. New York: Vintage Books, 1959, p. 4.
6. *Ibid.*, p. 6.
7. Marcuse, Herbert. *Eros and Civilization*. New York: Vintage Books, 1955, p. 7.
8. *Ibid.*, p. 13.
9. Becker, Ernest. *The Denial of Death*. New York: The Free Press, 1973, p. 34.
10. *Ibid.*, p. 26.
11. Becker, Ernest. *Escape From Evil*. New York: The Free Press, 1975, p. 163.
12. Roheim, Geza. *The Origin and Function of Culture*. New York: Anchor Books, 1971, pp. 122, 131.
13. Roheim, Geza. *The Gates of the Dream*. New York: International Universities Press, 1970, p. 595.
14. Freud, Sigmund. *Civilization and Its Discontents*, trans. Joan Riviere. London: Hogarth, 1975, p. 9.
15. *Ibid.*
16. Brown, Norman O. *Life Against Death*, ed. cit., p. xiii.
17. *Ibid.*, p. 126.
18. *Ibid.*, p. 280.
19. *Ibid.*, p. 290.
20. Brown, Norman O. *Love's Body*. New York: Vintage Books, 1966.
While Brown is considerably more aware in *Love's Body* than he is in the earlier volume of the significance of "introjection" in the foundation of the self (pp. 143-145), and in the development of cultural "alienation" as rooted in the attitude toward "property" (p. 145), he relies almost entirely for his "inspiration" upon the work of Melanie Klein. Although he talks of her "followers" (p. 143), they really are not present in the book with the exceptions of Heimann and Bion. As in *Life Against Death* the discussion as a whole is overwhelmingly centered upon *Freud and his followers*. This explains,

perhaps, why *Love's Body* is replete with theoretical presentations which do not jibe with the emphasis upon the early time, as it comes through the work of Klein. For example, the superego, as in Brown's earlier effort, is still fundamentally *paternal* (p. 144); there is no concentration upon its maternal roots and hence upon the relation of anxiety to guilt. Similarly, Brown's presentation of the psychodynamic issues that swirl around the existence of the state is predominantly patriarchal, echoing the writings of Freud, particularly *Moses and Monotheism*, and *Totem and Taboo* (pp. 10-21). The psychodynamics of familial organization are also presented from a Freudian perspective with the accent upon the brothers, upon *male* sibling rivals, upon the "dreaded primal *father*," the "male horde" (pp. 9-10, 17, *et. passim*). It is as if Brown's failure to *explore* the Kleinean development, to trace it into and through the work of followers such as Spitz, Jacobson, Fairbairn, and Winnicott, prevents him from seeing the *extension* of early psychodynamic problems into corresponding spheres of cultural life. The *infant's* world is Kleinean in *Love's Body*; the *social* world is still largely Freudian, with, once again, the curious exception of "property." This theoretical admixture makes for a confusing view of the "human experience."

21. Marcuse, Herbert. *Eros and Civilization*, ed. cit., pp. 69, 189.

22. *Ibid.*, p. 69.

23. Reich, Wilhelm. *The Mass Psychology of Fascism*, trans. Theodore P. Wolfe. New York: Orgone Institute Press, 1946. See also Reich's *Character Analysis*. New York: Orgone Institute Press, 1949. It should be stressed that Reich's union of Freud and Marx precedes Marcuse's, that Reich coined the term Freudo-Marxism, and that Marcuse is drawing on Reich, not the other way around. My organization here is as much rhetorical as it is historical; hence, the reversal.

24. Stein, Howard F. *Developmental Time, Cultural Space: Studies in Psychogeography*. Norman: University of Oklahoma Press, 1987.

25. Sagan, Eli. *At the Dawn of Tyranny*. New York: Alfred A. Knopf, 1985.

26. Stein, Howard F. *Developmental Time, Cultural Space*, ed. cit., p. 32.

27. Gesell, Silvio. *The Natural Economic Order*. London: Peter Owen, 1958, p. 32.

28. Greenacre, Phyllis. "The Transitional Object and the Fetish." *Psychoanalytic Quarterly*, XL (1971), 384-84. Reported by V. Fromberg.

29. Furnham, Adrian and Lewis Alan. *The Economic Mind*. Brighton: Harvester Press, 1986, p. 48. The emphasis here is added.

30. Freud, Sigmund. *Civilization and Its Discontents*, ed. cit., p. 1.

31. Becker, Ernest. *Escape From Evil*, ed. cit., p. 77.

32. *The Upanishads*. Trans. Juan Mascaro. London:Penguin,1965, p. 50.

33. See Wiseman, Thomas. *The Money Motive*. London: Hutchinson, 1974, p. 49.

34. See Brown, Norman O. *Life Against Death*, ed. cit., p. 246.

35. Desmonde, William H. "On the Anal Origin of Money." In *The Psychoanalysis of Money*, ed. Ernest Borneman. New York: Urizen Books, 1976, pp. 125-130.

36. Haddon, A. C. *A Survey of Primitive Money*. London: Methuen, 1963, p. 25.

37. Roheim, Geza. "Primal Forms and the Origin of Property." In Borneman, op. cit., pp. 153-163. (See note 35)

38. Erikson, Erik H. *A Way of Looking at Things: Selected Papers 1930-1980*. New York: W. W. Norton, 1987, p. 512.

39. Posinsky, S. H. "Yurok Shell Money and 'Pains.'" In Borneman, op. cit.,pp. 188-195. (See note 35)

40. Reich, Wilhelm. *Character Analysis*, ed. cit., pp. 90-91. (See note 23)

41. Roheim, Geza. *Psychoanalysis and Anthropology*. New York: International Universities Press, 1969, pp. 264-65.

42. *Ibid.*, pp. 181-82.

43. Hendy, Michael F. *Studies in the Byzantine Monetary Economy*. Cambridge, Eng.: Cambridge University Press, 1985, p. 272.

44. Roheim, Geza. *Psychoanalysis and Anthropology*, ed. cit., p. 228.

45. *Ibid.*, p. 268.

46. *Ibid.*, pp. 268, 275.

47. Bergler, Edmund. *Money and Emotional Conflicts*. New York: International Universities Press, 1959, p. 6.

48. *Ibid.*, pp. 6, 19.

49. Hubert, Henri and Mauss, Marcel. *Sacrifice: Its Nature and Function* [1898]. Chicago: University of Chicago Press, 1964, p. 9. I have added the emphasis. Subsequent references to this work will appear in the text with the abbreviation *S* followed by page number.

50. Schafer, Roy. *Aspects of Internalization*. New York: International Universities Press, 1968, ch. 8.

51. Einzig, Paul. *Primitive Money*. Oxford: Pergamon Press, 1951, pp. 72, 75. Subsequent references will appear in the text with the abbreviated form *PM* followed by page number.

52. Weber, Max. *The Protestant Ethic and the Spirit of Capitalism*. New York: Charles Scribner's Sons, 1958, p. 53.

53. Thomas Crump points out in his volume *The Phenomenon of Money* (London: Routledge Kegan Paul, 1981, p. 17) that "one discovers the origin of specie in precious ornaments which are brought out for display in certain rites de passage--generally related to birth, marriage, and death."

54. Huxley, Aldous. *The Perennial Philosophy*. New York: Harper and Row, 1970, p. 134.

55. Thomas Crump, op. cit., p. 179. (See note 53)

56. Neale, Walter C. *Monies in Society*. San Francisco: Chandler and Sharp,1977, pp. 14-16, 56.

57. Sagan, Eli. *At the Dawn of Tyranny*, ed. cit., p. 133.

58. Lenin, V. I. "Three Sources and Three Component Parts of Marxism." In *Karl Marx and Frederick Engels: Selected Works*. New York: International Publishers, 1968, p. 25.

59. Marx, Karl. *Das Kapital*, ed. Frederick Engels. Chicago: Charles H. Kerr, 1906, Vol. 3, p. 106. Subsequent references will appear in the text with the abbreviation *Kap* followed by volume and page number.

60. See Dylan Thomas' poem, *The Force that through the Green Fuse Drives the Flower*.

61. Marx, Karl. *Grundrisse: Foundations of the Critique of Political Economy*, trans. Martin Nicolaus. London: Penguin, 1973, p. 202.

62. Galbraith, John. *The New Industrial State*. New York: Mentor Books, 1972, pp. 34-35.

63. Kay, Geoffrey. *Political Order and the Law of Labor*. London: Macmillan, 1982, p. 125.

64. Harrington, Michael. *Socialism*. New York: Bantam, 1974, p. 37.

65. Galbraith. John. *The New Industrial State*, ed. cit., pp. 158-59.

66. Pederson-Krag, Geraldine. "A Psychoanalytic Approach to Mass Production." *Psychoanalytic Quarterly*, XXXI (1951), 445.

67. Offe, Claus. *Contradictions of the Welfare State*. London: Hutchinson, 1984, pp. 120, 143.

68. Weiss, Paul. *Toward a Perfected State*. Albany: State University of NewYork Press, 1986, p. 327.

69. Galbraith, John. *The New Industrial State*, ed. cit., p. 217.

70. *Ibid.*, p. 208.

71. *Ibid.*, p. 202.

72. *Ibid.*, p. 382.

73. Sagan, Eli. *At the Dawn of Tyranny*, ed. cit., pp. 375, 222.

74. Koenigsberg, Richard A. *The Psychoanalysis of Racism, Revolution, and Nationalism*. New York: Library of Social Science, 1977, p. 39.

Part Three

Disrupting the Tie

1. A Glance Backward, A Glance Forward

We have explored the infant's huge defensive capacity for internalization. We have noted the manner in which the object of the early period is taken deeply into the developing mind-brain, and into the human organism as a whole at the somatic level, to establish itself as a major structural facet of our emotional and bodily lives. Because the initial, primary object relation of mother and baby is filled with anxiety and frustration, as well as with bliss, the first years of life and the ordinary consciousness that arises therefrom are loaded with stress (the conversion process) and in particular, the *transitional stress* which expresses the child's life and death struggle to hold on to the object during the separation phase. We have come to understand how this stress finds its way projectively into the objects of the environment. Culture, in its discontentment, divisiveness, and aggression, and in its magical systems of support (the symbolic sphere), becomes a version of the split or divided inner realm; it renders both the positive and negative sides of the internalized caregiver, the side that nurtures and the side that hurts and disappoints. As we pointed out toward the close of the previous section, the first and chief domination of human experience is the domination of the individual by the objects within, the "immortal" objects whose persistent, implacable influence stands squarely behind those forms of domination that eventually characterize the social world in which the individual comes to have his "mature" existence.

The question now becomes, what can we do to ameliorate the situation? What can we do to improve our perceptual, emotional condition on the planet? How can we foster a sane, more equitable, less discontented civilization? In answering this, I would repeat again the major point: ordinary consciousness generally, in time, space, and language, is *itself* the transitional tie to the object of the early period. Thus the question, what can we do to ameliorate the situation, becomes in turn (and this is the revolutionary aspect of the matter) *what can we do to diminish or even sever the perceptual tie to the object? What can we do to alter our ordinary consciousness?*

This is, I admit, a strange and difficult notion. Our lives are so bound up with the objects of the inner realm and with the projective system of ordinary awareness which springs therefrom that the idea of getting away from these, of diminishing or terminating their influence, must appear problematical on the face of it, as if we would get out of our very psychic skins. We *are* our objects, and culture is their creation. That is pretty much all we know. Additionally, people haven't been thinking about doing this, about setting aside what is closest to them, their "normal" perceptual attitudes and tendencies. True, religious systems sometimes preach detachment from the world, but they also usually preach absorption in symbolic versions of the object, such as the body of Christ. The occident has witnessed a good deal of stoicism or psychological bearing up--detachment in that sense--as in the work of Freud or Philip Rieff; but this is merely more character armor and does not represent genuine mental and bodily change at all. It may be said of psychoanalysis in general that it is an incomplete tool of detachment, appealing primarily to the mind, or ego, and leaving the body and the senses out of the ameliorative picture. Certainly it does not see in everyday awareness the wellspring of the human malaise. Only the non-ordinary religions of the east (Buddhism, Sufism, Zen) appear to have grasped the extent to which suffering and alienation are rooted inextricably in our normative perceptual inclinations. I will soon have a great deal more to say of these valuable and intriguing disciplines; but even they appear to be deficient analytically, I mean deficient in grasping precisely the dynamic, developmental factors that load our ordinary consciousness with the life-consuming issues of the early period, and particularly the separation stage. What follows, then, is a preliminary attempt, made in a spirit of inquiry, to indicate a direction from which change might arise. I am not offering a cure-all; in my view, obviously, there is none. Nor am I suffused with expectation as I set about the task. The forces of the inner world are powerful, and people do not easily relinquish their mental habits, particularly when those habits tie them to the numinous, compelling figures of the past. Still, the potential for transformation may be there. It feels right to begin.

2. The Meaning of Non-Ordinary Moments

Often breaks with ordinary consciousness occur quite spontaneously, while one is jogging, or cooking, or dancing, or merely sitting still. My purpose in exploring briefly these "mystical" events is to alert the reader to their psychological significance *precisely as it emerges from the context of our discussion*. This will permit such happenings to be more consciously and more thoroughly appreciated than they perhaps presently are. Moreover, through the processes of unconscious association and suggestion, this heightened sensitivity may allow spontaneous breaks to occur with increasing frequency as joyous perceptual interludes leading to wholesale reorientation.

William James' *Varieties of Religious Experience* is loaded with representative examples.[1] A policeman strolls home after work in the evening and suddenly experiences a "spirit of infinite peace" and a "oneness" with the universe. He can hardly keep his feet on the pavement. A gentleman rides home in a cab after a night of philosophical discussion with friends. Suddenly he finds himself "wrapped in a flame-colored cloud" and undergoes a "sense of exultation," of "immense joyousness" and "intellectual illumination." A parishoner on the way to morning chapel leaves his wife and children on the road and strolls through a meadow by himself. As he returns, and again without warning, he feels that he is "in heaven," "bathed in a warm glow of light," and filled with "joy and peace." The objects around him "stand out more clearly," as if "nearer" than before.

A recent and strikingly similar account may be gleaned from a psychological case history presented by Dr. Paul Horton.[2] A patient attends church one morning after having fasted the previous day. Upon entering, she feels scared but soon finds herself quietly praying amidst the other worshippers. Suddenly a "brilliant white light" begins to shine within her. She feels radiant, "overcome with love and joy, . . . ecstatic." A few moments later the transport subsides. Ordinary consciousness, along with a certain sensation of "dullness," commences once more. Yet she knows that what has just happened to her is the "most real" event she has ever experienced. Horton maintains of this material that it discloses a "distortion of reality" insofar as the patient's "break" tends to "transmute outer events into inner experiences." As Horton views the matter, such distortion is accompanied by emotional regression, while the occurrence in its totality is ultimately dependent in nature: hungry, scared, and then "filled with light," the patient rediscovers the "good object," or the caretaker within.

I will not argue with Horton here. After all, the patient was his, and he offers a detailed analysis of her case. But it is worth mentioning that we are psycho-physical organisms who *always* perceive and feel at the same time. *Everyone* "transmutes the external event into the internal feeling." To do this is to be human. It is that simple. However, the majority of individuals, by the time they have reached adulthood, by the time they have fully endured the unconscious effects of infantile conversion, have very nearly *lost* this natural tendency. What often passes for objectivity or adherence to the reality principle is in actuality the deadening of one's sensitivity to the world. What Horton's patient undergoes as she sits radiant in church may contain not simply distortion but an element of integration. It may speak for an awakening capacity to attain an objectivity considerably more in touch with the reality of our emotional-perceptual style of existing than the constricted everyday awareness that is customarily regarded as normal. Thus to suggest, as Horton does, that breaks involve the rediscovery of one's good objects is acceptable only if one makes clear that the experiences cannot be equated with such a rediscovery. Depending upon the methods employed and the character of the experiencer, the ultimate result of transport may be increased integration and heightened awareness at all levels of personality.

To view breaks as always involving a rediscovery of the good object not only presents us with the danger of reductionism, it also presents us with the danger of psychological misemphasis, an equally serious error. While transport may involve fresh contact with the good presences within, that contact may actually be minimal in any given instance. Indeed--and here we reach a crucial point in our discussion--the quality of a break is frequently determined not by the degree to which the individual reparticipates in the good object, but by the degree to which he breaks free of internalized objects, good ones as well as bad ones. The question arises, how can this be? If the individual lessens or even severs the tie to internalized materials what is the source of his positive emotion? What is it that he recontacts? Surely his good feelings must originate somewhere; they do not come from the void. But in a very real sense, that is precisely where they come from. They are the result of the person approaching what is sometimes called his original nature, his being as it is given to him by those natural forces which created him. While the influence of the environment is, as we have seen, hugely significant, there is a genetical aspect of existence over which environmental influences are laid. In this way, there is an aspect of a break which is not derived from the world of the internalized other but which goes beyond or behind that world to a realm of experience in which vibrating atoms evolve along an infinite continuum of structural possibilities.

The relative presence or the relative absence of the good object in any given break will be determined, among other things, by the extent to which the individual who is having the transport experiences the diminution of time and space as we usually conceive of them, and the disappearance of symbols, or symbolical thoughts, as we usually conceive of them. One of James' subjects, for example, describes her "mystical interlude" as taking place during a solitary walk along the seashore. She feels liberated, reconciled with former enemies, closer to present friends, and impelled to kneel down before the "illimitable ocean," the "symbol of the infinite." The "earth," the "heavens," and the "sea," all "resound" as with "one vast . . . harmony." It is the conspicuous presence of the ocean as symbol which indicates the relative presence of the good object in this transport. Another instance in James is accompanied by a description which states, "there is no feeling, and yet the mind works, desireless free from restlessness, objectless, bodiless." The "alteration" stems "from the perception of forms and figures to a degree which escapes all expression." Or again, from a related account, "the soul finds no terms, no means, no comparison whereby to render the sublimity." One receives this "knowledge . . . clothed in none of the kinds of images . . . which our minds make use of in other circumstances."[3] Here we have, above all, the relative absence of the object. The tie to the inner world fades, diminishes, even disappears. One's perception is no longer objective in the double sense we are developing (the inner object projected into the external one). Such an experience, at first glance, might appear to resemble psychosis. But psychosis involves not the radical diminution or severing of ties to the inner world, as is sometimes thought to be the case. It involves, rather, the diminution or severing of only the good ties. The bad ones remain, as they do for J. A. Symonds who describes a spontaneous "trance" as consisting of a "gradual but swiftly progressive obliteration of space, time, sensation, and the multitudinous factors of experience, . . . the apprehension of a coming dissolution, . . . the abyss."[4] To put it somewhat differently, psychosis does not occur when the individual loses his connection with reality and can not, therefore, discover his way back to the ordinary universe. It occurs when the individual becomes absorbed into the bad object, when nothing remains but an inimical, persecuting presence.[5] Our job now is to grasp why the fading off of ordinary consciousness–time, space, symbol–should produce good, even joyous feelings, and how the diminution of these items may be triggered in the human organism.

3. The Emergence of the Non-Ordinary World

I will rely on Aldous Huxley's *Doors of Perception*[6] because it is the most vivid, powerful account of a break precipitated by the use of an hallucinogen. Before I begin, however, I will stress three points. First, Huxley's report is, in respect to its chief perceptual features, identical with other vivid, influential accounts by such writers as Havelock Ellis[7] and Christopher Mayhew.[8] Second, Huxley's pages look forward, once again in respect to perceptual items, to philosophical and religious utterances which stand at the center of the mystical tradition. Third, I am *not* advocating here the use of chemicals to achieve an altered state. In fact, I strongly discourage such usage. I include Huxley's account to emphasize that the changes in perception he experiences can be gained *without* the employment of mind-altering substances, as my second point above already implies.

Shortly after taking his pill, Huxley finds himself sitting quietly in his study and staring at a small glass vase that contains "three flowers--a full-blown Bell of Portugal rose, shell pink . . .; a large magenta and cream-colored carnation; and, pale purple at the end of its broken stalk, the bold heraldic blossom of an iris." Earlier that morning, at breakfast, Huxley had been struck by what he calls the "lively dissonance" of the flowers' hues. Now, however, he beholds something quite different, namely "what Adam had seen on the morning of his creation--the miracle, moment by moment, of naked existence." Continuing to behold the blooms in their living light, Huxley "seem[s] to detect the qualitative equivalent of breathing--but of a breathing without returns to a starting-point, with no recurrent ebbs but only a repeated flow from beauty to heightened beauty, from deeper to even deeper meaning." Words such as grace and transfiguration come to his mind, for as he perceives it, the experience he is undergoing indicates what such words stand for. Yet the "really important fact"--and here we reach the crucial perception with its tie to the infantile period--is that "spatial relationships" among objects cease of a sudden to "matter." The mind begins to apprehend in other than spatial categories. Instead of place and distance, "intensity of existence, profundity of significance," and "pattern" become paramount. Everything simply "glows" with a "living light."

After shifting his gaze to other objects and discovering their wondrousness--the "miraculous tubularity" of a nearby chair's legs for example--Huxley concludes from his "journey" that symbolic expression of the world's objects can only take one in the direction of "Suchness," never *to* it. An "emblem" such as Van Gogh's chair in the famous painting of his room is a "source of true knowledge about the Nature of Things, and this true knowledge may serve to prepare the mind which accepts it for immediate insights on its own account. But that is all." No matter how expressive they are, "symbols can never be the things they stand for." Art, then, "is only for beginners" or "for those resolute deadenders, who have made up their minds to be content with the *ersatz* of Suchness." Finally, one experiences in a break, in addition to the lessening of the ordinary sense of space, "some of the perceptual innocence of childhood when the sensum was not . . . automatically subordinated to the concept," as well as a diminution of the ordinary sense of time. As Huxley states it, "interest in time falls almost to zero."

The equation of a break, then, is clear: removed from ordinary space and time, as well as from symbolical thinking, the organism is suddenly filled with feelings of knowingness, wonder, and bliss, feelings that arise from a new, or altered, mode of perception. What underlies this process may be expressed this way: because symbolical sight depends upon a translation of the particular thing into an instance of the class of things to which it belongs in ordinary perception, symbolical sight perforce requires *duration*. There can be no translation without time. The brain subjects the impulses that stream toward it from the various receptors to a particular kind of analysis. It "refers the present moment of experience to its memory of the past and projects the past and present into the future, weighing the consequences of action not yet taken." When a decision is reached, the cortex "generates an integrated response" which is expressed in the action of the effectors or in the inhibition of action.[9] Input is never into a quiescent or static system, but always into a system which is already excited and organized, and behavior is always the result of the interaction of background with input. It is only when one can discern the characteristics of background that one can understand the effect of input.[10] Thus perceiving involves a *memory* that is not simply representational but related to the total organism.

The diminution of linear time which occurs in a break--when one is jogging, cooking, sewing, dancing, or merely sitting still--precludes or inhibits the formation of symbols. The thing which comes into the ken of the perceiver is apprehended directly rather than through re-cognition. We must bear in mind, here, of course, that re-cognition in psychology designates the reception of current feelings and/or events into mental sets which have been laid down during the early period, *the period in which the object is internalized in close and conflictual association to the development of temporal and spatial perception.* A chair, or a vase, or a flower, or a mountain is not unconsciously translated, in an instantaneous quantum burst of cerebral energy, into an *example* of the *species* chair or vase or flower or mountain. It becomes instead the creature that it simply is. Thus, without categories within which to fit items, the world is suddenly there, fresh, new pristine, with each perception of it. Again, because symbols live or exist in time, the time which permits the translation to occur, the apprehension of timelessness or the feeling of eternity will ordinarily increase with the diminution of symbolical sight. What I am describing is a kind of pulsation, a kind of reinforcing give and take, between the cessation of linear time and the direct perception of objects. As the items which comprise the external universe keep getting born anew, over and over again, eternity becomes real to the perceiver, as real as his own being, the organismic unit through which his perception transpires. "Believe it or not," declares Huxley, "eternity is real. It is as real as shit."[11]

However, if symbolical sight depends upon linear time for its existence, linear time, in turn, depends for its existence upon the continuous generation of cerebral or perceptual energy. "Perceptions are in quanta," says William James. "The concept of time as duration develops out of incessant impulses of voluntary reinforcement in maintaining attention with effort." Hence, "experience comes in quanta, and it is the intellect only that makes it continuous."[12] Freud's conclusions are virtually identical with James': the attention we bestow upon objects results from rapid but successive attractions which might be regarded in a sense as "quanta issuing from the ego." Inner perceptual action makes a continuity of such attractions only later. The "prototype of time" is found precisely here.[13]

Clearly then, the translation of thing into member of a class of things, a translation that is grounded in linear time and that constitutes the essence of ordinary awareness, is a particular kind of behavior, a particular kind of projective action, a specialized mental and emotional performance on the part of the human organism. As that behavior subsides, as that performance ends, the organism is suddenly charged with the very energy, the very quanta, that formerly went into the translation, into the making and maintaining of the temporal world and its symbolic inhabitants, the items of ordinary awareness. "The ubiquitous use of light as a metaphor for mystic experience may not be just a metaphor," suggests Arthur Deikman. "'Illumination' may be derived from an actual sensory experience involving the liberation of energy."[14] With the energetic connection between time and symbol firmly estalished in our minds, we are able to perceive the source of this liberation.

To stress the liberation of neurons is to stress what might be termed a physiological side of a break. To stress the manner in which this bears upon the internalized conflicts of the early period is to stress what might be termed a psychological side. Once again it is James and Freud who point the way. For when James writes that time as duration develops out of incessant impulses of voluntary reinforcement, and when Freud writes of the successive attractions which we bestow upon objects, each reminds us that ordinary awareness fulfils a *need* within the individual, a need which cannot be understood apart from its connection to the whole development of the person as a psychophysical organism. The voluntary maintenance of time as duration is rooted in the individual's need to translate the thing into the symbol and hence to retain the tie to the internalized object, to keep open the perceptual, psychological avenue which leads back to the parental figures. Because we answer the separation crises of infancy by internalizing the people we have to give up, and because the capacity for language, for symbolic thought, is the culmination of the internalizing process, a developmental feature that is actually goaded into operation by the anxiety surrounding separation, we cling to the symbolical mode of perception which arises from the early time and which provides us with the familiar, ordinary world.

But the translation of the thing into the symbol can only occur in time. Internalization, in other words, can only occur in time. In a sense, it *is* time. Hence, time as duration is voluntarily maintained by the individual because time as duration permits the translation upon which his ordinary emotional security rests. Needless to say, the accompanying spatial parameters which "house" the conceptualizations of everyday reality develop inwardly in close association to the symbols that keep appearing as the ordinary universe takes shape. Our space, in short, contains our time-bound words. We keep on making our temporal, spatial, symbolical world over and over again because just beneath it, we believe, lies the void, separation, isolation, oblivion. What psychologists call dual-unity, the ability to be separate from the object of infancy and yet, at the same time, to maintain contact, is grounded in the ability and the will to keep time going, for as long as time is kept going internalization, and the ordinary world of space and symbol which is its product, can also be kept going.

What one knows, deep down, in a break is that his well-being does not necessarily reside in his tie to the internalized object. The perceptual world that serves as a substitution for that object can be given up and one can still be all right. To be without one's linear time, one's ordinary space, one's habitual symbolic associations, one's obsessional postulation of the object through language, does *not* mean disaster. On the contrary, it means that one has a self which is not derived entirely from the mirror relationship and from the conflictual stages of separation that follow it. The love of the self, or the delight in the self, as we ordinarily experience it and conceive of it, is derived primarily from the caregiver's ministrations and affection. It is her love onto us which we transfer onto ourselves through internalization (and her frustration and anxiety too!). What we ordinarily take to be love of the self is in actuality love of the made self, the symbolical self, the self we can analyze and think about, the self that leads to the self-image, the reflection of the mirror, the ego. It is the conscious, heartfelt realization of precisely this point that can, through association and suggestion, find its way to our deepest levels of mind and thus stimulate a new perceptual attitude toward creation.

4.   Solidifying One's Change

Here I am interested in *practice*, practice designed to diminish the tension accumulated during the primary years and to foster a non-projective perception of objects, an alteration of the manner in which one apprehends not only the external environment but the world within oneself. Spontaneous breaks with ordinary consciousness will have beneficial effects upon the individual, and they offer us valuable insight into the psychological nature of so-called mystical experience. Yet they cannot, obviously, provide us with a complete foundation on which to build a program for genuine, lasting change. The awareness I plan to explore in the next few pages may be best achieved--and by best I mean most safely and conveniently--through techniques which fall under the heading of concentrative meditation, a complex, non-linear behavior involving bodily, emotional, perceptual, and cognitive alterations.[15]

The world of meditative practice offers us a wide variety of "schools," including several derived from Christian and Jewish sources. I will offer brief descriptions of four that, in my view, effectively underscore the perceptual aims of the context.

(1) Hindu Bhakti. Here the devotee, having removed himself to a quiet location and adopted a comfortable, sitting position, keeps the thought of his "ishta," or meditational object, foremost in his mind at all times. He may also repeat, mentally or aloud, the name of his ishta in a rhythmic, concentrative way. By bringing his mind to one-pointedness through the constant remembrance of the ishta, the practitioner reaches the first level of meditative consciousness. Subsequently he experiences a lessening of the need to cling to the external form of his devotional object. The states that it once evoked become the fixtures of his own awareness. Concentrating upon pure being as it begins to manifest itself internally, the meditator proceeds along the path of spiritual evolution.[16]

(2) Transcendental Meditation. The best known meditational technique in the west, TM asks its practitioners to follow the classic Hindu mantra meditation, that is, to meditate upon a brief word or phrase derived from Sanskrit sources. Examples might be "Shyam," a name of Lord Krishna, or "Aing," a sound sacred to the Divine Mother. Instructed to avoid effortful concentration by bringing his mind back

gently to the mantra as it wanders, the student narrows his attention, eventually reaching more and more subtle levels of thought until his mind transcends the experience of the subtlest state of thought and arrives at the source of thought. With steady, long-term practice, one enhances his ability to experience objects through the senses while at the same time maintaining his essential nature, his "being."[17]

(3) Sufism. The chief meditational practice of this school is called *zikr*, which means remembrance. The seeker attempts to overcome the mind's natural state of carelessness and inattention through an oral repetition which later becomes silent. The most eminent and influential *zikr* is, translated, "there is no god but God." According to the Sufis, ordinary human consciousness comprises a kind of sleep in a nightmare of unfulfilled desires. With transcendence, which is brought about by not letting one's attention wander for the duration of a single breath, this nightmarish condition gives way to what is termed by Indries Shah "objective consciousness," an extra dimension of being that operates concomitantly with normal or everyday cognition.[18]

(4) Zen. Here one's training commences with a firm grounding in concentration. Sitting quietly in an effort to achieve a state of oneness in which the differences between things dissolve, the seeker concentrates upon his *koan* (a mental puzzle without a rational solution) or upon his breathing. The principal fruit of successful practice is *satori*, a profound awakening during the course of which one sees into his true nature. Paradoxically, it is the empty mind one achieves through meditation that provides the power to gain this special sight. We must remember here that *satori* does not signify trance-like dullness, but a brilliantly clear state of mind in which the details of every phenomenon are perceived, yet without evaluation or attachment. In the ultimate Zen condition of no mind the intuitive clearness of satori infuses itself into all of one's action. Means and ends come together.

Distilling this material for a general understanding of practice, I would suggest that it *commences* in the choice of a quiet location, the adoption of a relaxed yet straight-backed posture, and the focusing of attention with the accompanying renunciation of stimuli, and *consists* in a regularized training of awareness aimed at modifying mental processes so as to elicit enhanced states of consciousness and well-being.[19] As for the explicitly religious aspect of the ancient technique, I would set it aside in keeping with my conviction that such activity comprises, in part, the human species' intuitive attempt to reduce the psychobiological tension of the infantile period, specifically the mirror and separation phases. We are now in a position to employ such practice in a conscious, secular manner, to get from it what we will. In precisely this spirit, let us begin to examine at length the physiological and psychological implications of this methodology.

5. Transforming the Past at the Mind-Body Level

We must recognize from the outset that we are dealing with the human mind, not simply with the human brain, and that the distinction is fundamental. True, our behavior is composed to a considerable extent of automatic responses to sensory inputs. However, to understand the "motivations that underlie our actions" we must know something of the "genetic determinants, cultural elements, and intercerebral mechanisms" that are involved in various kinds of behavioral performance.[20] More specifically, because all mental functions are related to inner or outer stimuli, because mind can manifest itself only in behavior, and because the mind cannot exist without a functioning brain, we can conclude that the mind is linked, necessarily, to stimuli, to behavior, and to the brain. Without stimuli, the mind cannot exist, and without behavior, it cannot be recognized. In this way, mind may be defined as the intercerebral elaboration of extracerebral information, and the focus is on the origins, reception, dynamics, storage, retrieval, and consequences of this information. In the words of Jose Delgado (at which we looked in Part One), "mind is born early in life as an infant is attracted to sources of comfort and repelled by sources of distress."[21] Such experiences lead to the intelligent recognition of objects and persons associated with positive and negative reinforcement, and they will determine selective patterns of behavioral response.

The origin of mind, then, is pinpointed at precisely the time in which the infant begins to interact with the objects (both good and bad) that will enter integrally into his mental structure. It must be stressed that such structure cannot be understood, developmentally or motivationally, apart from these objects. There is no mind, there can be no mind in any genuine, human sense, without the fundamental internalizing activities of the early period. Hence, if practice has something to do with the mind in a hard, physiological way, and if the mind is crucially determined by the internalizations we have been describing, then practice *has also to do with these internalizations*. As Gerald Edelman points out in his book *Neural Darwinism*, when the brain learns something it experiences physical changes.[22] Because the related problems of projective perception and neurotic discontent are linked inextricably to this mind-brain through the stimuli of the primary years an answer to those problems may reside here, at the structural level where the split object of the early period shapes the developing human *will*, guides the developing human personality in a way that has its consequences in the symbolic, cultural universe which, in turn, lends its stimulation to the creature. It will help to recall in this connection the nature of human memory, particularly the very close tie between retrieval and sheer stimulation.

Memory functions as essentially a two-step process. A stimulus such as a smell, or touch, or image arouses a person's short-term memory which then resonates through the immense complexity of the brain until an association is triggered in long-term memory. The correspondence between an immediate sensory stimulus and a portion of a stored memory instigates the retrieval of the entire stored memory. This is because the brain is ultimately a holographic structure, that is to say, a structure with the property of storing the whole in each part, each part being capable of generating the whole.[23] Experiments involving laboratory rats, for example, have indicated that memory is retained intact if just one small segment of the brain remains intact.[24] Additional striking support for this view has come from the work of Pietsch who established that the brain function of salamanders remained sound in spite of wholesale alteration, and even obliteration, of their brain tissues.[25] Specific memories are incredibly resistant to brain damage.

For our purposes, however, the most compelling evidence derives from the work of Wilder Penfield.[26] I realize, of course, that certain of Penfield's conclusions have recently been challenged.[27] Still, the overall thrust of his research is unmistakable. Operating upon a girl of fourteen for epilepsy, a girl whose attacks were invariably preceded by a traumatic, hallucinatory recollection from her seventh year in which a strange man asks her to crawl into a bag filled with snakes, Penfield discovered that electrical stimulation of the cortex of the temporal lobe reproduced the hallucination. Furthermore, when the electrode was held in place, the memory disclosed itself sequentially, as in a film. The cause of this young woman's seizures was discovered to be a portion of brain that had been damaged during infancy. The scarring that had developed with the passage of time was precipitating the fits. As to why those fits were invariably preceded by a recollection of the fright she underwent in her seventh year, Penfield maintains that the injured area was triggering the memory that had been formed with the occurrence of the psychological trauma, and it was this area that he was able to arouse with the electrode.

Anthony Campbell writes of this material that it offers us "direct experimental evidence of a severe stress having been recorded in the cortex" and reminds us that "it is not necessary for a conflict to be present in awareness if it is to produce effects." True, our estimation of this particular case is complicated by the epilepsy caused by the earlier brain damage, but "even if there had been no brain damage the experience would still have been recorded and might well have given rise to nightmares and other behavioral disturbances."[28] Penfield's subsequent explorations confirm this conclusion.

Through the employment of electrical implantations in a wide variety of individuals, Penfield has been able to disclose not only the regions of the cortex that "have a particular relationship to the record of experience, and to the reactivation of that record," but the fact that all experiences to which human beings have paid attention form "ganglionic patterns" which remain "intact and available to the stimulating electrode" in later years. From the "cries of other children, to the honking of horns, to the barking of dogs," the stimuli with which we are touched as we live our lives remain embedded and resonating in the folds of our mind-brains. "Every individual," concludes Penfield, "forms a neuronal record of his own stream of consciousness, from childhood to the grave."[29]

Let us call to mind here a few related points established in the context: first, infants and children have robust memories; second, the child's perception of the environment and of himself is inextricably associated with his caretaker, to whom he is constantly paying attention; and third, unconscious fantasy provides the mental set in which sensory stimuli are perceived and integrated. Clearly then, at the deepest levels of mind, *all stimuli are received in the context of the first relationship*, including the mirror and separation phases with their anxiety, terror, expectation, and bliss. The good and bad experiences of the initial, split stage of life become the foundational, ganglionic *a priori* of all that subsequently happens to us simply because mind is in large measure stimuli and all stimuli are able to recall, or to reactivate, the object of the primary years with which they were originally fused. In the links between the stimulus, the internalized object, the mind, and the memory we reach the very bone level of the stress in our bones. Merely being sentient, merely receiving stimulation, can be anxiety-provoking to the anxious animal that we are.

We grasp from this perspective the psychological significance of that *renunciation of stimuli* and *focusing of attention* which reside at the heart of the meditative tradition. Ornstein writes that "continuous repetition of the same stimulus [the "ishta" or "mantra" for example] may be considered the equivalent of no stimulation at all. Concentrative meditation is a practical technique which uses an experimental knowledge of the structure of our nervous system to 'turn off' awareness of the external world."[30] Thus, the techniques of concentrative meditation are not deliberately mysterious or exotic but are simply a matter of practical applied psychology. Similarly, Deikman contends that the "deautomatization of response" upon which the "alteration of awareness" depends may be straightforwardly induced by "renunciation," specifically the renunciation of sensorial input or stimuli.[31] We may now add that *concentrative meditation is a practical technique which uses psychological knowledge of the structure of the psyche to moderate the tie to the internalized object upon which one's ordinary perception of the world is automatically and conflictually based.*

We also grasp from this angle the analytic significance of that "empty mind" which stands as the highest philosophical and spiritual achievement of the meditative tradition. Writes Shunryu Suzuki, "when you have something in your consciousness you do not have perfect composure. The best way toward perfect composure is to forget everything. Then your mind is calm, and it is wide and clear enough to see and feel things as they are without any effort. Actually, emptiness of mind is not even a state of mind, but the original essence of mind which Buddha experienced."[32] To the degree that one lessens his tie to the internalized object he empties his mind. As we have seen, the world of ordinary awareness, the world of ordinary time and space, the world of ordinary symbolical thinking, was achieved in the effort to retain that tie. The very running on of our thoughts became our habitual way of preserving our security. That is why it is so difficult to stop the running on. When the tie to the object is eased we are able to see the variety and the freshness of the world because we no longer need to see that, or primarily that, which reestablishes and reconfirms our bond to the object within. What the infant experiences during the mirror and separation phases is learned in his organs, in his muscles, in his chemistry, in his visceral brain. To internalize the caretaker in response to specific early traumata is to internalize her into the body-ego where she will continue to lodge, and to dictate our perceptual style, until the sort of change we are describing here occurs. What we take to be our normal perception is in actuality a conflicted mind-body system of belief that can be modified significantly through a practice that reaches down to the foundational, organic levels with their accumulated tension and stress. Thus the peaceful body one attains during meditation is the somatic equivalent of the empty mind. To relax is to stop one's bodily thoughts, to sever the connection with the early period at the unconscious, bodily level, the level of physiological processes. That such relaxation should go hand in hand with a perceptual change is perfectly natural when we recall once again that ordinary consciousness, consciousness in time and space and symbol, is the outgrowth of physical processes, and the means of retaining the tie to the object within. To *receive* the stimulus in an altered bodily condition is to *perceive* the world in a new, non-ordinary way.

With regard more specifically to the rhythmic aspects of meditation which are manifested in the repetition of the "mantra" or in the concentration upon breathing, we note that "rhythm has been universally recognized as a natural tranquilizer, with regularly repeated sounds or rhythmic movements spontaneously used to quiet agitated infants." If "contacting deep biological rhythms in oneself is a prominent component of meditation, then regular meditation might be expected to have a deeply soothing effect."[33] Such an effect has been measured in a wide variety of well known studies, recounted by Walsh, in which the EEG patterns of meditators have displayed a considerably higher frequency of alpha waves than those of non-meditators.[34] It is not without significance to observe in this connection that such frequency *increases* with practice.[35] Further studies also employing EEG measurements have suggested that meditative concentration promotes a synchronized functioning of the brain's right and left hemispheres.[36] Summarizing the empirical research, Walsh maintains that the benefits of practice may include, "relaxation, deconditioning, heightened awareness, and facilitation of psychological development and maturation."[37]

As for perceptual changes, they are obviously more difficult to measure, but we do have a fascinating paper contributed by Brown and Engler in which it is specified that advanced meditators responding to the Rorschach cards "actually witness energy/space in the moment-by-moment process of arising and organizing into forms and images; and conversely, witness the forms and images becoming absorbed back into energy/space." By contrast, meditators in the beginning stages respond with the customary projective versions of persons and objects, the "normal" situation.[38] In my view, such a result not only supports Carrington's contention that meditation gives rise generally to a "withdrawal of projections,"[39] but deepens the meaning of Garfield's discovery that "long-term meditation" is an "effective tool" for the "reduction of the individual's level of death-fear."[40] As we noted in Part One, the fear of death is inextricably tied to the traumata of the separation phase and in particular to the bad object that we internalize during the course of that phase. At their deepest pathological ground, *our projections are born here.* Hence, to encourage a perceptual condition in which projections tend to be withdrawn is to encourage a state in which the fear of death will be lessened. Can anyone fail to discern the importance of such a development for the human species whose endless appetite for destruction and violence may well be rooted in its furious wish to deny the reality of a death that is unconsciously equated with the catastrophes of the infantile period? I cannot think of a more compelling consideration with which to bring our discussion to a close. To diminish the perceptual tie to the object within may well be the only way for the forces of life to win the old, grievous battle with the forces of death.

A concluding word: in her fine, provocative essay on mysticism, Marion Milner emphasizes "the importance of direct, non-symbolic internal awareness of one's own body from the inside," the "ongoing background matrix of one's own being which can yet become foreground once one has learned the skill of directing attention to it." [41] The purpose of this last chapter, and in some sense of this monograph as a whole, has been to underscore the integral connection between the "awareness of one's own body from the inside" and methodologies designed to truncate the somatic-perceptual tie to the object of the inner realm. The developmental psychology of this century, particularily psychoanalysis, culminates in our understanding of the extent to which the projective, stress-filled madness that passes for reason in our world is linked etiologically to the internalizations of the early period. Such madness may be equated with a "normal," ordinary consciousness located squarely in the symbolic mode and longing for a "mystic" reorientation that would give the body a more central place in the perceptual scheme than it currently enjoys. We've been brought to a crossroad. We've been forced to realize that the very ground of our being--the internalized object of life's first years--is the source of our discontentment and malaise. Just where we will go from here is, of course, the vital question.

Notes and References

Part Three

1. James, William. *The Varieties of Religious Experience* [1902]. New York: New American Library, 1958, pp. 302-305.
2. Horton, Paul. "The Mystical Experience." *Journal of the American Psychoanalytic Association*, 22 (1974), 364-380.
3. James, William. *The Varieties*, ed. cit., pp. 304, 311.
4. *Ibid.*, p. 296.
5. Aronson, Gerald. "Defence and Deficit Models." *International Journal of Psychoanalysis*, 57 (1977), 11-16.
6. Huxley, Aldous. *The Doors of Perception*. London: Penguin, 1974, pp. 16-26.
7. Ellis, Havelock. "Mescal: A New Artificial Paradise." In *The Drug Experience*, ed. David Ebin. New York: Grove Press, 1961, pp. 225-236.
8. Mayhew, Christopher. "Peyote." In *The Drug Experience*, ed. cit., pp. 293-306.
9. See Kleitman, Nathaniel. "Patterns of Dreaming." In *Altered States of Awareness*, ed. Timothy Teyler. San Francisco: W. H. Freeman, 1972, pp. 44-50.
10. See Lashley, K. S. "The Problem of Serial Order in Behavior." In *Brain and Behavior*, ed. Karl H. Pribram. London: Penguin, 1969, Vol. 2, pp. 515-540.
11. See Huxley, Laura. *This Timeless Moment*. New York: Ballantine Books, 1971, p. 132.
12. See Eisenbrath, C. R. *The Unifying Moment: The Psychological Philosophy of William James and Alfred North Whitehead*. Cambridge, Mass.: Harvard University Press, 1971, pp. 143, 264.
13. See Bonaparte, Marie. "Time and the Unconscious." *International Journal of Psychoanalysis*, 21 (1940), 467. Freud's views appear in a footnote written specifically for this paper.
14. Deikman, Arthur. "Deautomatization and the Mystic Experience." In *The Nature of Human Consciousness*, ed. cit., p. 227.
15. See Kornfield, Jack. "Intensive Insight Meditation." *Journal of Transpersonal Psychology*, 11 (1979), 41-58.
16. I am indebted here and in the following descriptions to Daniel Goleman's *Varieties of Meditational Experience*, New York: E. P. Dutton, 1977, pp. 45ff.
17. See Maharishi, Mahesh Yogi. *The Science of Being and the Art of Loving*. Los Angeles, SRM Publications, 1966, p. 53.

18. Shah, Indries. *Wisdom of the Idiots*. New York: E. P. Dutton, 1971, p. 62.

19 . See Walsh, Roger. "A Model for Viewing Meditation Research." *Journal of Transpersonal Psychology*, 14 (1982), 69-84.

20. Delgado, Jose. *Physical Control of the Mind*. New York: Harper and Row, 1971, p. 9. I am indebted here and in the following paragraph to Delgado's work.

21. *Ibid.*, p. 46.

22. Edelman, Gerald M. *Neural Darwinism*. New York: Basic Books, 1987, p. 45.

23. Pribram, Karl H. "What the Fuss is All About." In *The Holographic Paradigm*, ed. Ken Wilbur. Boulder: Shambhala, 1982, p. 32.

24. Pelletier, Kenneth. *Toward a Science of Consciousness*. New York: Delta, 1978, p. 120. I am indebted throughout this paragraph to Pelletier's splendid explanation of memory which I follow very closely.

25. Pietsch, Paul. "Shuffle Brain." *Harper's Magazine*, May 1972, pp. 41-48.

26. Penfield, Wilder and Rasmussen, T. *Cerebral Cortex of Man*. New York: Macmillan, 1950, pp. 164-167.

27. Hunt, Morton. *The Universe Within*. New York: Simon and Schuster, 1983, pp. 109-110.

28. Campbell, Anthony. *The Mechanics of Enlightenment*. London: Gollancz, 1975, p. 102.

29. Penfield, Wilder and Roberts, Lamar. *Speech and Brain Mechanisms*. Princeton: Princeton University Press, 1959, pp. 48, 51.

30. Ornstein, Robert and Naranjo, Claudio. *On the Psychology of Meditation*. New York: Viking, 1972, p. 169.

31. Deikman, Arthur. "Deautomatization and the Mystic Experience." In *The Nature of Human Consciousness*, ed. cit., p. 225.

32. Suzuki, Shunryu. *Zen Mind, Beginner's Mind*. New York: Weatherhill, 1973, pp. 128-129.

33. Carrington, Patricia. "Meditation Techniques in Clinical Practice." In *The Newer Therapies*, ed. Lawrence E. Abt and Irving R. Stuart. New York: Van Nostrand Rheinhold, 1982, p. 69.

34. Walsh, Roger. "Emerging Cross-Disciplinary Parallels." *Journal of Transpersonal Psychology*, 11 (1979), 166.

35. *Ibid.*

36. Earle, Jonathan. "Cerebral Laterality and Meditation." *Journal of Transpersonal Psychology*, 13 (1981), 155-173.

37. Walsh, Roger. "A Model for Viewing Meditation Research." *Journal of Transpersonal Psychology*, 14 (1982), 69-84. For a similar summary see Dubs, Greg. "Psycho-Spiritual Development in Zen Buddhism." *Journal of*

Transpersonal Psychology,19 (1987), 32.

It may also be of interest to note here Hekmat's finding that concentrative meditation had the effect of improving psycho-somatic difficulties which were traceable to tensions originating during the early period and in particular during the separation phase, such as stuttering. See Hekmat, Hamid. "Instructional Desensitization." *Psychotherapy*, 22 (1985), 273-280.

38. Brown, Daniel P. and Engler, Jack. "The Stages of Mindfulness Meditation." *Journal of Transpersonal Psychology*, 12 (1980), 143-192.

39. Carrington, Patricia. "Meditational Techniques in Clinical Practice." In *The Newer Therapies*, ed. cit., p. 68.

40. Garfield, Charles. "Consciousness Alteration and Fear of Death." *Journal of Transpersonal Psychology*, 7 (1975), 147-175.

41. Milner, Marion. *The Suppressed Madness of Sane Men*. London: Tavistock Publications, 1987, p. 263.